Knowing God by Heart

Knowing God by Heart

*An Invitation
To a Praise-Driven Life*

Joy Thornton

© 2007 by Joy Thornton. All rights reserved.
2nd Printing 2014.
www.joythornton.org

Trusted Books is an imprint of Deep River Books. The views expressed or implied in this work are those of the author. To learn more about Deep River Books, go online to www.DeepRiverBooks.com.

No part of this publication may be reproduced, stored in a retrieval system or transmitted in any way by any means—electronic, mechanical, photocopy, recording or otherwise—without the prior permission of the Publisher, except as provided by USA copyright law.

Unless otherwise noted, all Scriptures are taken from the Holy Bible, New International Version, Copyright © 1973, 1978, 1984 by the International Bible Society. Used by permission of Zondervan Publishing House. The "NIV" and "New International Version" trademarks are registered in the United States Patent and Trademark Office by International Bible Society.

Scripture references marked KJV are taken from the King James Version of the Bible.

Scripture references marked NASB are taken from the New American Standard Bible, © 1960, 1963, 1968, 1971, 1972, 1973, 1975, 1977 by The Lockman Foundation. Used by permission.

Reprinted from The Attributes of God Volume 1 with Study Guide by A.W. Tozer, copyright © 1997, 2003 by Zur Ltd. Used by permission of WingSpread Publishers, a division of Zur Ltd., 800.884.4571.

Reprinted from The Attributes of God Volume 2 with Study Guide by A.W. Tozer, copyright © 2001, 2003 by Zur Ltd. Used by permission of WingSpread Publishers, a division of Zur Ltd., 800.884.4571.

From THE KNOWLEDGE OF THE HOLY: The attributes of God: Their Meaning in the Christian Life by A.W. Tozer. Copyright © 1961 by Aiden Wilson Tozer. Reprinted by permission of HarperCollins Publishers.

ISBN 13:978-1-63269-366-2
Library of Congress Catalog Card Number: 2006907316

Table of Contents

Introduction vii

1. God Is Unchanging 14
2. God Is Forgiving 20
3. God Is Loving 28
4. God Is Faithful 34
5. God Is Omniscient 42
6. God Is Omnipotent 48
7. God Is Omnipresent 54
8. God Is Holy 60
9. God Is Compassionate 68
10. God Is Victorious 76
11. God Is Just 84
12. God Is Trustworthy 90
13. God Is Merciful 96
14. God Is Eternal 102
15. God Is Sovereign 108

16. God Is Relational 114
17. God Is All-wise 120
18. God Is Good 128
19. God Is Generous 136
20. God Is Perfect 142
21. God Is Truthful 150
22. God Is Accessible 156
23. God Is Extravagant 162
24. God Is Loyal 168
25. God Is Gracious 174
26. God Is Creative 180
27. God Is Majestic 186
28. God Is Infinite 192
29. God Is Patient 198
30. God Is Gentle 204
31. God Is Impartial 210

Endnotes 217

Introduction

As our family sat in the car loaded with our most precious treasures, I looked at the home I loved and wondered why God was leading us to move across the country. We were happy in our neighborhood, in our city, and in our church. We enjoyed wonderful friends. Life was comfortable.

After the long road trip, I dove into my new surroundings, trying to feel at home again. As much as I tried, I only felt more overwhelmed. Frustration turned to fear and depression. I worried about my children trying to adjust to a new school and find new friends. My city road map wasn't accurate and I kept getting lost. I wondered if I would find my niche again. This new chapter in my life was not what I had hoped it would be, and my mood sank as winter approached.

One morning as I told God how terrible my life had become, I realized my complaining was a dead-end street.

I needed to turn my worry into praise. Instead of fear and hopelessness, I needed to build my faith by praising the Lord. Although I didn't feel like it, I began to say, "I exalt you, Lord. I praise you. I worship you. You are good." I too soon ran out of praise words. I didn't know what else to say. For what else could I praise God? What else did I know about him? What else could I say to express my praise and worship?

I drew a set of grids on a blank sheet of paper, one square for each day of the month. Then I wrote a word in each box—something I knew to be true about God. As I read my Bible and came across a Scripture that confirmed that attribute, I listed the reference in the box also. My pain gave way to praise.

For Christians, praise is a powerful weapon in spiritual warfare. Praise is simply recognizing God for who he is and giving him the glory for it. When we worship God, we express our appreciation for him. The basis of our praise is declaring God's character and his attributes. The Greek word for praise, *epainos*, indicates commendation. To "commend" means to represent as worthy or to express approval. When we praise God, we show our approval and admiration for whom he is. It's like complimenting him. Through praise we can experience great power with God. Praise brings us into God's presence.

Each person has a distinct personality and so does God. His attributes make him who he is. If you were asked to describe the personality of a friend, you might use words like "loyal," "humorous," or "caring." Our personalities consist of the characteristics or attributes that make us uniquely

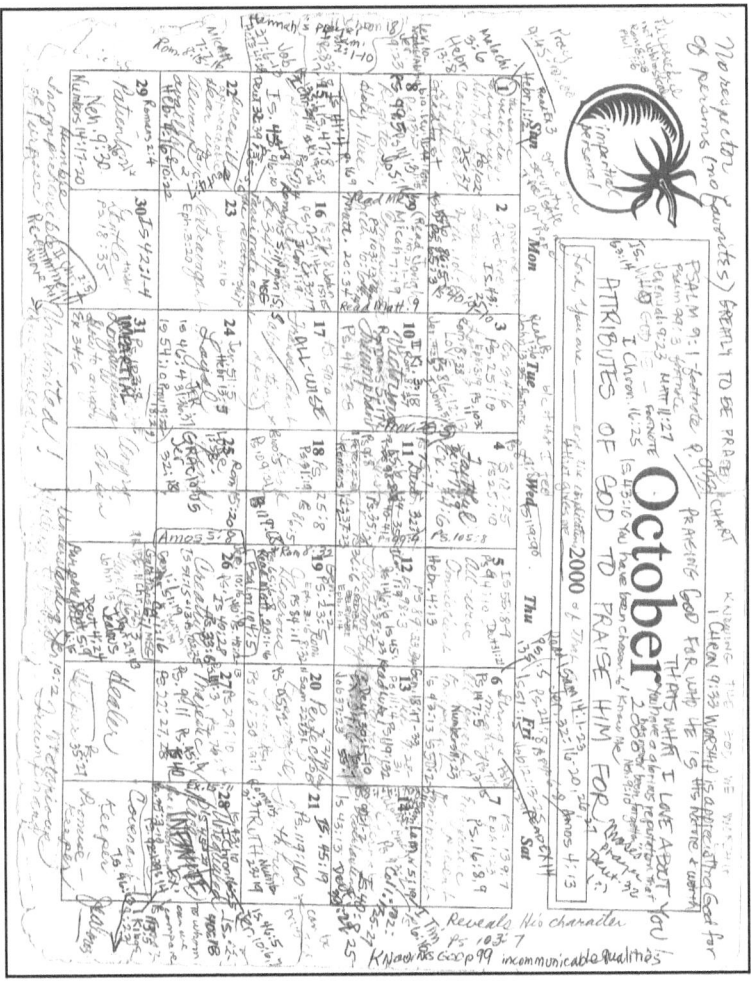

who we are. Although God is incomparable and we cannot fully understand him, he has chosen to reveal himself to us. He has done this through Jesus and through his Word.

A.W. Tozer said what we think about God is the most important thing about us: "That our idea of God correspond as nearly as possible to the true being of God is of immense importance to us."[1] When wrong ideas about God enter our minds, we begin to doubt God's capabilities. We secretly wonder if we can trust him. We think God isn't fair or that he has forgotten about us. Worries increase, and fear has a heyday in our minds. At that point, we have played right into Satan's hand. Anytime he can minimize God's character to us, he has scored. Thoughts about God not loving us or not being big enough to handle our situations come directly from the Evil One. "If we would bring back spiritual power to our lives, we must begin to think of God more nearly as he is."[2] To live a life of security and wholeness and peace, we must begin to have a right concept of God. Our confidence comes in thinking proper thoughts of him and expressing our admiration.

As you focus on who God is, your own needs will be met. When you're under stress, praise God because he is good. When you're feeling insecure, understand that he is sovereign. When you're sad, praise God because he is faithful. When you're lonely, remember God is omnipresent. When you're fearful, knowing who God is will offer peace. Knowing and praising God for who he is will build your faith—and faith is the antidote to fear. Faith is simply confidence in God.

How does a person get to know God? It's a lot like getting to know others from a human perspective. You begin to enjoy each other's company. You listen to them and they listen to you. You come to find out what they like and what they don't. You begin to share deep thoughts and secrets with each other. You think about each other when you're apart. You miss being together. It's out of a relationship like this that trust and appreciation grow. Our relationship with God isn't as mystical as we sometimes make it. It's a lot like getting to know a good friend.

> But the people who know their God shall prove themselves strong and shall stand firm and do exploits [for God].
> —Daniel 11:32 AMPLIFIED

In his book *Knowing God*, J. I. Packer shares four characteristics of a person who truly knows God. First, Packer says that person will have great energy for God. Are you excited to spend time in prayer and in God's Word? Second, that person will have great thoughts of God. What is your life saying about how you view God? Are you trusting in his faithfulness and his incredible power? Are you in awe of his unlimited greatness and his holiness? Third, a person who truly knows God will show great boldness. Are you allowing our culture to press you into its mold or are you determined to take a godly stand no matter what the cost? Fourth, this person will have great contentment. Is your life filled with regrets and what-ifs or do you find peace in remembering God is governing your circumstances?

We think we need our problems solved. What we really need is a more accurate view of God. On the following pages are some of God's attributes. Each attribute is a handle for worship. Each one is a reason to praise him. The thirty-one chapters can be used as a perpetual calendar month after month. I love waking up in the morning and before opening my eyes worshiping God for the attribute listed on that particular day. Then through the day, I watch for how God shows himself to me in this and many other ways!

Several months after I changed my approach to life, my circumstances hadn't changed, but I had. Confidence in God's sovereignty invaded my spirit and I began to rest in his power over circumstances. His unconditional love for me became real and I trusted him to be faithful to keep his promises. As you read this book, think about how his attributes affect your life and your situation.

We were made to know and worship God. Let God reveal himself to you through his Word. It's better to know God than to know the answers to our problems. Think great thoughts of him—God loves, God knows, and God can! He's waiting for you to learn more about him. Turn the page and begin.

> "This is what the LORD says: 'Let not the wise man gloat in his wisdom, or the mighty man in his might, or the rich man in his riches. Let them boast in this alone: that they truly know me and understand that I am the LORD who is just and righteous, whose love is unfailing, and that I delight in these things. I, the LORD, have spoken!'"
> —Jeremiah 9:23-24 NLT

Knowing God by Heart

God, I Praise You because You are...

Sun	Mon	Tue	Wed	Thu	Fri	Sat
1 Unchanging Malachi 3:6	2 Forgiving Psalm 86:5	3 Loving Psalm 103:11	4 Faithful Psalm 105:8	5 Omniscient Psalm 94:10	6 Omnipotent Psalm 147:5	7 Omnipresent Psalm 139:7
8 Holy Isaiah 5:16	9 Compassionate Psalm 103:13	10 Victorious Romans 8:37	11 Just Psalm 9:4	12 Trustworthy Psalm 9:10	13 Merciful Titus 3:5	14 Eternal Colossians 1:17
15 Sovereign Isaiah 46:10	16 Relational John 15:15	17 All-wise Jeremiah 10:12	18 Good Psalm 100:5	19 Generous Romans 8:32	20 Perfect Psalm 27:4	21 Truthful Isaiah 45:19
22 Accessible Psalm 86:7	23 Extravagant Ephesians 3:20	24 Loyal Hebrews 13:5	25 Gracious John 1:14	26 Creative Psalm 104:5	27 Majestic Psalm 45:4	28 Infinite Job 36:26
29 Patient Romans 2:4	30 Gentle Psalm 18:35	31 Impartial Romans 2:11				

Chapter 1

GOD IS UNCHANGING

All that God was and is, God will ever be. His nature and attributes are eternally unchanging.[1]
—A.W. Tozer

Unchanging: remaining the same; showing or undergoing no change.

Synonyms: consistent, enduring, immutable, invariable, permanent, perpetual, same, unvarying.

But you are always the same; your years never end.
—Psalm 102:27 NLT

It's in God's plan for each of us to become more like him: more compassionate, more forgiving, more loving. However, there are some ways we can't be like God. He has incommunicable qualities—characteristics we do not and cannot share, because he is God. For instance, he is present everywhere, all-powerful, and unchanging.

His character doesn't change. His ways, his purposes, and his truth never change. He doesn't change his mind. He is stable, consistent, fixed, in everything he says and does.

"I am the Lord and I do not change."
—Malachi 3:6 NLT

We are a different story!

We change our minds almost as easily as we change our clothes. I read a letter to *Dear Abby* from a dad who does the laundry in his home. He complained that his seven-year-old daughter changed her clothes so often he seemed to be washing her entire wardrobe every week. Some people change their minds like they change their clothes!

Or we can't make up our minds. One afternoon my mother and I went shopping and we each bought a dress. That evening we changed our minds and we both returned our dresses.

A person's character can change, sometimes due to difficult circumstances. A good-natured person can become cynical. A kind person can become bitter. A trusting person can grow sour.

Our words change. I can say something and then forget I said it or change my mind about what I said. We've all had to eat our words at times when we realized we had spoken too soon or we were just plain wrong. Sometimes I change my opinion. When new information comes to me, I may see things differently. My emotions also change—sometimes unpredictably! Just ask my husband.

The fact that people change is painful. Someone may smile at you one day and ignore you the next time. People disappoint us, treat us poorly, change how they feel about us, and leave our heads spinning because of what they say or do.

God does not change. This is completely different from the way we are made. Change is certain with us; it is not possible with God. God is not created. He is independent and self-sufficient and will always be. God announced his changelessness when he declared his name to Moses: "I AM THAT I AM."

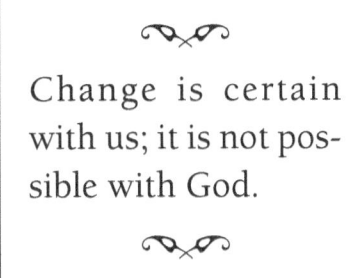

Change is certain with us; it is not possible with God.

Nothing about God will ever change. Nothing will change God's words to us. He will never forget what he has spoken. He will never change his thinking about us. Nothing we do or don't do will ever change how he feels about us: absolute love.

God is holy and eternal—and he can't get any better or worse than that! There's nothing relative about God. He simply *is*! Whatever he thought about you, he still thinks. Whatever he said and promised, it's still good.

> Every good and perfect gift is from above, coming down from the Father of the heavenly lights, who does not change like shifting shadows.
> —James 1:17 NIV

There used to be a TV commercial with the Rock of Gibraltar as its symbol. The message was that the item was something you could depend on, something immoveable that will always be there. Fine, that's a rock—but I'm talking about God, who can actually do something for you!

Whatever God has said, he still means. Whatever he has done, he will do again. If you need to see things more clearly, he is the same Jesus who made the blind see. He'll feed you as he fed the crowds. If you need peace, he'll calm you as he calmed the sea. He'll forgive you as he forgave the woman who fell at his feet. He'll give you eternal life as he gave it to the man on the cross beside him.

What does this mean for us? There is ultimate security and rest through all the changes and uncertainties of life in our dependable, unchanging God.

I Praise You Because You Are Unchanging!

Read more about God declaring himself the unchanging one in Exodus 3.

Questions for Reflection

Recall a time you changed your mind about something. What was the outcome?

Has someone changed in his or her actions toward you? What was the result?

What do you need from God that he has done for others in the past?

What does it mean to you that God does not change?

Pray

God, I am thankful that you do not change. When my circumstances are changing, I can depend on you to always stay the same. Even when those closest to me disappoint me, I can count on your unchanging love. I find great security in knowing your good plans and purposes for me do not vary. With a grateful heart, Amen.

Related Verses

And he who is the Glory of Israel will not lie, nor will he change his mind, for he is not human that he should change his mind!
— I Samuel 15:29 NLT

His unchanging plan has always been to adopt us into his own family by bringing us to himself through Jesus Christ. And this gave him great pleasure.
— Ephesians 1:5 NLT

Jesus Christ is the same yesterday, today, and forever.
— Hebrews 13:8 NLT

Chapter 2

GOD IS FORGIVING

The sins of God's children do not destroy their justification or nullify their adoption, but they mar the children's fellowship with their Father.

—J. I. Packer[1]

Forgiving: willing or able to forgive; to pardon or overlook the wrongful acts of another person.

Synonyms: pardon, relieve, excuse.

I have told everyone the good news that you forgive people's sins. I have not kept this good news hidden in my heart, but have proclaimed your loving-kindness and truth to all the congregation.

—Psalm 40:9-10 TLB

When Faye was planning her wedding, her sister Betty became angry over an ethical decision Faye made. Faye's choice did not sit well with Betty. Although Faye explained the reason for her action, Betty would not forgive her. Years went by and Betty continued to talk to others about Faye's decision concerning the wedding. After more than fifty years Betty was still holding a grudge and chose to cut off communication with her sister. Faye wrote her letters, only to have them returned unopened.

Have you ever been around someone who held a grudge? It's not a pleasant place to be. The offended person continues to bring up reminders of the past offense. When we dredge up the ugly past, this is evidence of our inability to forgive. Someone said, "The more I get to know the human race, the more I love my dog." Dogs forgive and forget easily. People often do not.

> For all have sinned; all fall short of God's glorious standard.
> —Romans 3:23 NLT

Because of Adam and Eve's sin, it is in our nature to sin. All of us have failed God—we have refused to do what God wanted or rebelled against him. Our sin separates us from God, so we need his forgiveness.

God is able and willing to pardon us. He is the only one who can cancel our debt of sin. It is part of his loving nature. Forgiveness is instantaneous when we ask God for it and repent sincerely. To "repent" means to change from rebellion against God to acceptance of his will and lordship in our lives. The Amplified Bible defines *repent* this way: "to change your mind for the better, heartily amend your ways with abhorrence of your past sins." When we repent, we reestablish the broken relationship with God due to our sin. It is amazing that God so freely forgives us, but in addition he totally forgets our sin.

> "I—yes, I alone am the one who blots out your sins for my own sake and will never think of them again."
> —Isaiah 43:25 NLT

> He has removed our rebellious acts as far away from us as the east is from the west.
> —Psalm 103:12 NLT

The east and the west can never meet. This symbolism shows us that God will never bring up a sin from the past. He will never remind us of a sin we would like to forget. That means he will never hold a grudge because he does not remember our sin.

> He [the Holy Spirit] will convince the world of its sin.
> —John 16:8 NLT

The Holy Spirit gently convicts us when sin is present in our lives. This is part of the Holy Spirit's role. That convincing, or conviction, is always gentle. When the memory of a sin continues to resurface after we have asked Christ for forgiveness, the Evil One is at work trying to drive condemnation into our hearts. Condemnation and guilt are never from God.

> So now there is no condemnation for those who belong to Christ Jesus.
> —Romans 8:1 NLT

The cycle of sin leading to repentance and forgiveness is meant to strengthen us, not weaken us. When condemnation interrupts that cycle, we get stuck. Believe that God forgives you and determine to live in the victory God provides.

> The cycle of sin leading to repentance and forgiveness is meant to strengthen us, not weaken us.

> But if we confess our sins to him, he is faithful and just to forgive us and to cleanse us from every wrong.
> —I John 1:9 NLT

When we try to live right but continue to commit the same sin, it is easy to become discouraged. God understands our weaknesses and the areas of our lives that are difficult for us to gain victory. When we are sincerely struggling, God stands ready to help us with those vulnerable areas. However, if we continue to sin and justify it, that is entirely different. Genuinely repent and ask for the Holy Spirit's help in conquering your weaknesses. True repentance means you will make the needed corrections in your life. Deal with the root issue that is causing the sin so you do not give the devil room to maneuver in your life. When repentance is sincere, it leads to a change in your attitudes and behavior.

Forgiveness is God's promise to us. Accepting it is our responsibility. Confessing our sins and accepting God's forgiveness is meant to lighten our cares and bring us freedom. When we ask God for forgiveness, we do not need to beg. We do not need to ask for forgiveness again and again once we have asked. Believe that God has totally forgiven you. God is bigger than our fears. His forgiveness is complete. We are secure in his love.

I Praise You Because You Are Forgiving!

To read more about God's forgiveness, read Psalm 32 and Psalm 51.

Questions for Reflection

What is your response to God's offer of forgiveness?

Is there a particular sin with which you are struggling? What are some steps you can take toward overcoming it?

Has guilt or condemnation interrupted the repentance cycle? What will you do about it?

God is generous in his forgiveness. How will you demonstrate forgiveness to others?

Pray

Gracious Father, help me to be quick to ask for your forgiveness when sin is in my life. I don't want to live separated from you. I humbly admit my sin and ask you to forgive me. Thank you for cleansing me and removing my sin from your memory. May I walk in freedom. Amen.

Related Verses

"No matter how deep the stain of your sins, I can remove it. I can make you as clean as freshly fallen snow. Even if you are stained as red as crimson, I can make you as white as wool."

—Isaiah 1:18 NLT

O Lord, you are so good, so ready to forgive, so full of unfailing love for all who ask your aid.

—Psalm 86:5 NLT

Lord, if you kept a record of our sins, who, O Lord, could ever survive? But you offer forgiveness that we might learn to fear you.

—Psalm 130:3-4 NLT

Chapter 3

God Is Loving

God's love is an exercise of his goodness towards individual sinners whereby, having identified himself with their welfare, he has given his Son to be their Saviour, and now brings them to know and enjoy him in a covenant relation.[1]

—J.I. Packer

Loving: feeling love; affectionate; indicative of or exhibiting love.

Synonyms: affectionate, attentive, caring, concerned, kind, tender, thoughtful.

God told them, "I've never quit loving you and never will. Expect love, love, and more love!"

—Jeremiah 31:3 MESSAGE

No strings attached! Lifetime guarantee! Most of the time these kinds of offers sound too good to be true. *"Come and spend three days at our beachfront resort and simply attend a one-hour presentation."* Aha—but there was a catch, a condition, attached. In life we often assume the same is true.

God's love has no strings attached. It is unconditional—absolutely unqualified.

God's love is not like human love. The nature of God's love is completely different than the way we love. Without realizing, we can slip into thinking patterns about God and his love that are incorrect.

God does not give or withhold love based on our performance as people sometimes do. In a USA Today poll 63 percent of parents said their children's behavior definitely affected or somewhat affected what they received for Christmas.[2] In other words, if you are good you will be rewarded.

There is nothing we can do to make God love us any more or any less than he does now. God's love has nothing to do with how good we have been. God doesn't love only those who love him back. His love isn't based on feelings. He simply chooses to love us. Just look at the action his love prompted.

We don't have to fully understand God's love before we accept it. It is vitally important that we *do* accept it, though. Take some time alone with God and thank him for loving you. Let his genuine love sink deep into your spirit. He loves you "just because." Maybe you haven't experienced unconditional love from a parent or a spouse. Maybe you don't think you deserve to be loved. Just think: God, who is perfect, loves you. That certainly makes you worth loving!

> May your roots go down deep into the soil of God's marvelous love. And may you have the power to understand, as all God's people should, how wide, how long, how high and how deep his love really is. May you experience the love of Christ, though it is so great you will never fully understand it.
>
> —Ephesians 3:17-19 NLT

Accepting God's love is the basis for our relationship with him. As we continue to let our roots go down into his love, changes will begin to happen in us.

The apostle John and his brother James were called the Sons of Thunder for a reason—they had a boisterous bent (Luke 9:49, 54). You know, the kind of people who enter a room "mouth first!" After spending time with Jesus and accepting his love, John was changed. When he realized how much he was loved, John, in turn, was able to love others. He wrote five New Testament books. In I John 4 he writes:

> Dear friends, let us continue to love one another, for love comes from God. Anyone who loves is born of God and knows God. But anyone who does not love does not know God—for God is love. God showed how much he loved us by sending his only Son into the world so that we might have eternal life through him. This is real love. It is not that we loved God, but that he loved us and sent his Son as a sacrifice to take away our sins.
> —I John 4:7-10 NLT

What are some of the changes we can expect when we truly believe God loves us? Confidence will replace fear. Contentment with our present circumstances will replace resentment. Passion for God will replace a half-hearted loyalty. When insecurities begin to surface, focus again on God's immeasurable love for you. There is nothing so healing as knowing that God loves you unconditionally.

When an antique is appraised, the appraiser uses many criteria to determine the worth of the item. The item's age, its origin, and its condition are all taken into account when trying to arrive at the price the object is worth. Even after the research is done, antique appraisal is still an imprecise, subjective business rather than a science. The dollar value placed on an item is only an estimate because the question remains: at an auction, what is someone willing to pay for it? Only then is the true value known.

>
> There is nothing so healing as knowing that God loves you unconditionally.
>

The worth of an item is determined by who sees value in it. The homeliest vase can bring thousands of dollars if there is a buyer who wants it. It's amazing what some attic-worn items are worth. Even more amazing is the response of the surprised owner!

Our worth is based on the fact that God loves us. He was willing to pay the ultimate price for us—the life of his Son, Jesus.

I Praise You Because You Are Loving!

For further reading on God's love, read I John 3 and 4.

Questions for Reflection

Describe what God's unconditional love means to you.

Let the thoughts you wrote settle in your mind. Have you truly accepted that you are of incredible worth to God?

How has your outlook changed as the result of accepting God's love?

How will you show love to someone today?

Pray

Dear God, your love for me is so great I cannot fully comprehend it. You have assured me that your love will never end and it will never be withdrawn. You see such value in me that you gave Jesus to die for me. Help me to show my gratefulness by the way I live. Thank you for your amazing love. Amen.

Related Verses

> There is no fear in love [dread does not exist], but fullgrown [complete, perfect] love turns fear out of doors *and* expels every trace of terror! For fear brings with it the thought of punishment, and [so] he who is afraid has not reached the full maturity of love [is not yet grown into love's complete perfection].
>
> —I John 4:18 AMPLIFIED

For the LORD your God has arrived to live among you. He is a mighty savior. He will rejoice over you with great gladness. With his love, he will calm all your fears. He will exult over you by singing a happy song.

—Zephaniah 3:17 NLT

For his unfailing love toward those who fear him is as great as the height of the heavens above the earth.

—Psalm 103:11 NLT

Chapter 4

GOD IS FAITHFUL

Upon God's faithfulness rests our whole hope of future blessedness. Only as he is faithful will his covenants stand and his promises be honored.[1]

—A.W. Tozer

Faithful: steadfast in affection or allegiance; adhering firmly to promises or in observance of duty; worthy of trust; implies unswerving adherence to a person or thing or to the oath or pledge or promise by which a tie was contracted.

Synonyms: trustworthy, constant, steadfast, devoted, true.

Your unfailing love, O Lord, is as vast as the heavens; your faithfulness reaches beyond the clouds.

—Psalm 36:5 NLT

Building a home is a fascinating process. One of the subcontractors hired to work on our home was unfaithful. He said he would be on the job on a certain day and he didn't show up. He said he would finish by a certain date and he didn't. He said he would charge a certain amount and, again, he did not keep his word.

Faithfulness speaks of a person's character. As the dictionary definition says, a faithful person is firm in sticking to his promises. In years past, a handshake finalized a contract. It was all that was needed to seal a deal. A person's

character determines whether he will be true to what he has said he will do. Some people boast about their plans and talk about their ambitions, but they don't follow through on what they have said. Some people promise to show up, to be on time, or to return something they have borrowed. It doesn't happen. Promises that were meant to be lifelong are broken and become a source of great heartache. When a person promises to do something and fails to do it, his name begins to have a sour taste in your mouth. He can't be counted on! But a faithful person keeps his promises, even when it hurts.

> Putting confidence in an unreliable person is like chewing with a toothache or walking on a broken foot.
> —Proverbs 25:19 NLT

God's promises are guaranteed. Faithfulness is a cornerstone of God's being. In Revelation 19:11 (NLT), God calls himself "faithful and true." God makes thousands of promises to us in his Word, and we can depend on each of them.

> Faithfulness is a cornerstone of God's being.

> I will give thanks to your name for your unfailing love and faithfulness, because your promises are backed by all the honor of your name.
> —Psalm 138:2 NLT

> O LORD God Almighty! Where is there anyone as mighty as you, LORD? Faithfulness is your very character.
> —Psalm 89:8 NLT

For over ten years I have kept a "Thankful Journal"—a record of God's faithfulness—which my family reads at our Thanksgiving dinner table. Throughout the year I record answers to prayer, large and small. We read about protection from accidents, unusual provision, healings, and finding lost things. One year we had driven 1,800 miles on a trip. As soon as we arrived at our destination, the car's brakes failed. Another entry told of when our daughter, home from college for Christmas, felt prompted to give some money in a special offering. In February, she received an unexpected check in the mail for the same amount she had given. We know these events are not coincidences. This is God's protection, his provision, and his surprises at work in our lives. This is overwhelming evidence of God's faithfulness and his character on display.

In what ways has God promised to be faithful? When we repent of our sin, he promises his faithfulness.

> If we confess our sins, he is faithful and just and will forgive us our sins and purify us from all unrighteousness.
> —I John 1:9 NIV

When we are discouraged, he is faithful to give us the strength we need.

> But the Lord is faithful, and he will strengthen and protect you from the evil one.
> —I Thessalonians 3:3 NIV

Even when we are not faithful to God, he is faithful to us.

> If we are faithless [do not believe him and are untrue to him], he remains true [faithful to his Word and righteous character], for he cannot deny himself.
> —II Timothy 2:13 AMPLIFIED

He is faithful when we are tempted. He will not allow us to be pushed past our limit in temptation.

> But remember that the temptations that come into your life are no different from what others experience. And God is faithful. He will keep the temptation from

becoming so strong that you can't stand up against it. When you are tempted, he will show you a way out so that you will not give in to it.
—I Corinthians 10:13 NLT

So if you're discouraged, worried, fearful, tempted—whatever your need—God has a promise for you. To anything he has spoken, God will stand by it. He will be true to whatever he has said.

Without wavering, let us hold tightly to the hope we say we have, for God can be trusted to keep his promise.
—Hebrews 10:23 NLT

All your commandments are faithful and sure.
—Psalm 119:86 AMPLIFIED

For someone who is completely devoted to you and will always be true to what he has said to you, great praise is in order. A pagan king who learned that God is faithful spoke the following words. I challenge you to say your name instead and praise God for his faithfulness in your life.

Now I, Nebuchadnezzar, praise and extol and honor the King of heaven, whose works are all faithful and right and whose ways are just.
—Daniel 4:37 AMPLIFIED

I Praise You Because You Are Faithful!

For further reading on God's faithfulness, read Psalm 106.

Questions for Reflection

Write what the word *faithful* means to you.

Look back at your life and think about the times you saw God's faithfulness. Record one of those situations.

Find a promise in God's Word that speaks to your present situation.

What does it mean to you knowing that God is completely faithful?

Pray

Precious Lord, forgive me for the times I have doubted your faithfulness. Even though people have not always kept their promises, thank you for reminding me that you always will. Thank you that you are faithful even when I am not. Help me to claim the words you have spoken for my situation and remember that your promises are guaranteed. I praise you for your faithfulness! Amen.

Related Verses

He always stands by his covenant—the commitment he made to a thousand generations.
—Psalm 105:8 NLT

God is faithful [reliable, trustworthy, true to his promise, dependable]; by him you were called into companionship and participation with his Son, Jesus Christ our Lord.
—1 Corinthians 1:9 AMPLIFIED

Faithful is he who is calling you [to himself] and utterly trustworthy, and he will also do it [fulfill his call by hallowing and keeping you].
—1 Thessalonians 5:23-24 AMPLIFIED

Chapter 5

GOD IS OMNISCIENT

He knows in one free and effortless act all matter, all spirit, all relationships, all events.[1]

—A.W. Tozer

Omniscient: having total knowledge; knowing everything.

Synonyms: all-seeing, almighty, infinite, knowledgeable, pre-eminent, wise.

Who is able to advise the Spirit of the LORD? Who knows enough to be his teacher or counselor? Has the LORD ever needed anyone's advice? Does he need instruction about what is good or what is best?

—Isaiah 40:13-14 NLT

Cynthia Heald puts it this way:
God knows what he is doing. He has his ways for you, and they are higher and better than what you would settle for on your own. They bring him glory and accomplish his purposes in your life. He longs to show himself mighty on your behalf. He wants you to know that his ways are always best, even though they may appear to be bewildering or unfair."[2]

Have you listened to your local weather forecaster lately? We rely on him or her to know whether it will be warm enough for that dinner on the deck, if rain will threaten our outdoor plans, or whether a freeze endangers our flowers outside. But they are often wrong. It doesn't rain after all. The temperature dips low enough to destroy those delicate plants. Despite our education, technology, and skill, no person can predict perfectly one second into the future.

How wonderful it is that God knows everything. Not only does he know facts, he knows thoughts and intents. He sees through every motive. He knows everything about the future. He knows the dynamics of each relationship because he knows the thoughts and motives of each person involved.

When we're making decisions, God knows all the ramifications of one choice or another. It is important to trust him because he knows everything about the people and circumstances in a situation. His love, omniscience, and goodness interact on our behalves if we trust him.

> "My thoughts are completely different from yours," says the LORD. "And my ways are far beyond anything you could imagine. For just as the heavens are higher than the earth, so are my ways higher than your ways and my thoughts higher than your thoughts."
> —Isaiah 55:8-9 NLT

When God closes a door, we should trust him because he knows the outcome already and is always acting in love toward us.

Learn to look beyond the present and trust that God sees the big picture.

Instead of complaining that you didn't get your way, thank God for protecting you. His delay is not denial. All we can see is a part of the picture. Learn to look beyond the present and trust that God sees the big picture.

> Nothing in all creation can hide from him. Everything is naked and exposed before his eyes. This is the God to whom we must explain all that we have done.
> —Hebrews 4:13 NLT

Trust your all-knowing God. He knows you perfectly. He knows what is best for you. He knows your deep inner desires and your dreams, even the ones you are not able to verbalize. He understands your frustrations and disappointments and acts in love for you even though you do not understand his ways at times.

> And Solomon, my son, get to know the God of your ancestors. Worship and serve him with your whole heart and with a willing mind. For the LORD sees every heart and understands and knows every plan and thought. If you seek him, you will find him.
> —I Chronicles 28:9 NLT

I Praise You Because You Are Omniscient!

For further reading on God's omniscience read Daniel's prayer in Daniel 2:20-23.

Questions for Reflection

Who is the smartest person you know?

List some of the things God knows that you could not possibly know.

Write about a time when you prayed for something and God in his omniscience had a different solution for you.

What are you currently facing that you need to place in God's hands?

Pray

Lord God, because you have only good in mind for me, I can totally trust my life to you. You know the future and I accept your greater purposes for me even when I don't understand them. What security I have in recognizing that you have total knowledge of my life and my situation. I praise you! In your name, Amen.

Related Verses

> [Earnestly] remember the former things, [which I did] of old; for I am God; and there is no one else; I am God, and there is none like me. Declaring the end from the beginning, and from ancient times the things that are yet done, saying, my counsel shall stand, and I will do all my pleasure and purpose.
> —Isaiah 46:9-10 AMPLIFIED

> He knows everything—doesn't he also know what you are doing?
> —Psalm 94:10 NLT

Oh, what a wonderful God we have! How great are his riches and wisdom and knowledge! How impossible it is for us to understand his decisions and his methods! For who can know what the Lord is thinking? Who knows enough to be his counselor? And who could ever give him so much that he would have to pay it back? For everything comes from him; everything exists by his power and is intended for his glory. To him be glory evermore. Amen.

—Romans 11:33-36 NLT

Chapter 6

GOD IS OMNIPOTENT

Your need is nothing compared with the great things that God has done.[1]

—A.W. Tozer

Omnipotent: having unlimited or universal power, authority, or force.

Synonyms: almighty, supreme, unlimited, unrestricted.

For the LORD is the one who shaped the mountains, stirs up the winds, and reveals his every thought. He turns the light of dawn into darkness and treads the mountains under his feet. The LORD God Almighty is his name!

—Amos 4:13 NLT

Who has the ability to leap tall buildings with a single bound? Fly through the air with amazing speed? Superman, of course! Although his role was fictitious, *Superman* actor George Reeves was overcome by it. He took his own life in 1959, reportedly because he felt helplessly typecast as Superman. Powerful "Superman" could not help himself.

Our lives are a statement of what we think about God. The way we live shows what we think about him. So what do you think about God? Do you believe that he is all-powerful—omnipotent?

Psalm 147:5 says: "How great is our Lord! His power is absolute!"

—NLT

God has the ability and the capacity to perform any function. He has all the energy and might needed to carry out any task. All power belongs to God and originates with him. Nothing is too hard for God. In our unbelief, we don't ask God to intervene in situations we think might be too hard even for him. Is it a problem in a relationship? Do you need healing? Is it a habit you can't break? A problem too complicated to figure out? God can do anything!

>
> In our unbelief, we don't ask God to intervene in situations we think might be too hard even for him.
>

God is also omniscient. He knows everything: facts, thoughts, motives, reasons, the future, all the implications of past actions, what we need and when. He knows what we're trying to tell him when we can't get it out. He is God!

If God was just powerful but not wise, we might have trouble. You probably can name some powerful people who aren't very smart. If God had all wisdom without the power, that wouldn't be a lot of help either.

God also loves us perfectly—better than the best parent or spouse could love anyone. And it isn't just that God is loving—God IS love. We might say that his love overlaps all his other attributes, so that God can't do anything that is not done in love. His love isn't conditional. He'll never love you any more or any less than he does right now.

God always thinks about you lovingly. Even if he disciplines us or allows hardships, it's his love that allows it. Have you ever allowed your child to experience the consequences of an action so he or she will learn from it? We have no reason to be afraid of God's love.

God loves us perfectly. He knows everything and he can do anything! There is every reason to trust someone like that.

When we don't see God answer our requests according to our schedules, the Enemy floods our minds with questions about God: his faithfulness, his ability, his love for you. Satan wants you to be impatient, to make you fearful, to convince you that God is not able to do something so big, and that God is too slow and he's ignored you.

> I pray that you will begin to understand the incredible greatness of his power for us who believe him. This is the same mighty power that raised Christ from the dead and seated him in the place of honor at God's right hand in the heavenly realms. Now he is far above any ruler or authority or power or leader of anything else in this world or in the world to come.
>
> —Ephesians 1:19-21 NLT

Years ago I heard a talk titled "God Is Greater Than I Thought He Was." Our individual experiences color our concepts of God. At some time you may have felt God didn't love you or he let you down or disappointed you.

Satan's main desire is to minimize the greatness of God in your eyes. But God is powerful and can do what you're asking him.

I tell you, God is greater than you think he is!

> You are the God of miracles and wonders! You demonstrate your awesome power among the nations.
> —Psalm 77:14 NLT

I Praise You Because You Are Omnipotent!

Read a story of God's power in Exodus 14.

Questions for Reflection

Do you believe God can do anything? Have you ever had a problem you thought was too hard for God?

When a problem arises do you tend to trust your own strength first or God's? If you trusted yourself, what was the outcome?

We live according to our view of God. How is your life reflecting your trust in God's omnipotence?

What are the obstacles in your life for which you need God's power?

Pray

Mighty God, I celebrate your unlimited power. I praise your almighty strength. Thank you that your strength is available for my problems. There is absolutely nothing too hard for you. I'm so glad that whatever I'm facing I can turn to you for help. In your name, Amen.

Related Verses

"I am the Lord, the God of all the peoples of the world. Is anything too hard for me?"
—Jeremiah 32:27 NLT

I know the greatness of the LORD—that our Lord is greater than any other god.
—Psalm 135:5 NLT

Then the Lord said to Moses, "Is there any limit to my power?"
—Numbers 11:23 NLT

Chapter 7

GOD IS OMNIPRESENT

The knowledge that we are never alone calms the troubled sea of our lives and speaks peace to our souls.[1]
—A.W. Tozer

Omnipresent: present everywhere simultaneously; divine attribute equivalent to immanent; implies being so active or so numerous as to seem to be found everywhere.

Synonyms: ubiquitous, immanent.

I know the Lord is always with me. I will not be shaken, for he is right beside me. No wonder my heart is filled with joy, and my mouth shouts his praises! My body rests in safety.
—Psalm 16:8-9 NLT

Even in a crowded shopping mall or a cheering stadium, many people feel alone. Loneliness is the state of being without companions. It is desolate and solitary. It can bring a haunting sense of dejection. These types of emotions can bring an insecurity that eats away at us on the inside. These are lies brought to you by the Enemy of your soul.

David's confidence and security was found in the truth that God was always with him.

> I can never escape from your spirit! I can never get away from your presence!
>
> —Psalm 139:7 NLT

This is a wonderfully comforting fact. God is present everywhere at once—he is omnipresent. He is with everyone, everywhere.

Whether you feel him or not isn't the point. Even David felt distant from God at times. Whether you are physically alone or surrounded by people, God is there with you. How we underestimate this truth! We tend to live by emotions rather than fact. We know that God is with us, that he sees us and knows us. Are you dreading a trip you have to make or a meeting you must attend? Whom are you concerned about today? God knows where they are. Knowing that God is with each of us wherever we are should give us great security.

While I was on a missions trip halfway around the world, my family was at home and one of our daughters had just moved across the country. As a mother, I wanted my family together. I find security in that. However, children go to school, grow up, and move away from us. Loved ones pass away. Friends are busy with their own lives. It's not always possible to be together. Sometimes the loneliness we feel is due to more hurtful circumstances, like rejection

The key to contentment and freedom from fear is to recognize that God is with us wherever we are and under any circumstances.

or abandonment. In those times, we may feel there is no one to turn to.

But when we know God, we know we are never alone. The key to contentment and freedom from fear is to recognize that God is with us wherever we are and under any circumstances. He sees you.

> The Lord looks from heaven, he beholds all the sons of men; From his dwelling place he looks upon all the inhabitants of the earth.
> —Psalm 33:13-14 AMPLIFIED

He is that big! Read Psalm 139 and think about God's unlimited presence. You cannot get away from his presence. If you love God, that is good news!

> In thy presence is fullness of joy.
> —Psalm 16:11 KJV

If you're tired of being around someone, you can stand up and leave the room. You can leave the presence of other people but you can never leave the presence of God. As you read Psalm 16, notice that God's presence brings guidance (verse 7), protection (verse 8), and joy (verse 9). David found contentment by meditating on God's unlimited presence. The next time you feel alone, remember that God is with you. Practice his presence. Sit still and quietly and thank him that he is always with you. Thank him that you can never be away from his gentle care. Thank him that he is with your family and friends whom you can't be with at the moment. That is when his presence and joy begin to fill us.

If you are God's child, you can never move out from under the umbrella of God's care and guidance. Because God's presence is everywhere, his love, his power, his strength, and his comfort are everywhere. Because of this we can echo the words of the apostle Paul:

> And I am convinced that nothing can ever separate us from his love. Death can't and life can't. The angels can't and the demons can't. Our fears for today, our worries about tomorrow, and even the powers of hell can't keep God's love away. Whether we are high above the sky or in the deepest ocean, nothing in all creation will ever be able to separate us from the love of God that is revealed in Christ Jesus our Lord.
> —Romans 8:38-39 NLT

We base our lives not on our circumstances, but on the truth that God is always with us.

I Praise You Because You Are Omnipresent!

For further reading, read Psalm 139.

Questions for Reflection

Can you remember a time you felt alone?
What will God's omnipresence mean for you the next time you feel alone?
What is the difference between knowing God is with you factually and feeling his presence?

How can you be more aware of God's presence?

Pray

Precious Father, I know you are always with me. You are closer to me than any person could be, closer than my own thoughts. Help me to recognize your presence and rest in it. Thank you for the peace and joy I experience in your presence. I praise you. Amen.

Related Verses

> Even when I walk through the dark valley of death, I will not be afraid, for you are close beside me.
> —Psalm 23:4 NLT

> Then Jacob woke up and said, "Surely the LORD is in this place, and I wasn't even aware of it."
> —Genesis 28:16 NLT

> You hide them in the shelter of your presence.
> —Psalm 31:20 NLT

Chapter 8

GOD IS HOLY

He is absolutely holy with an infinite, incomprehensible fullness of purity that is incapable of being other than it is.[1]

—A.W. Tozer

Holy: regarded with or worthy of worship or veneration; revered; specified or set apart for a religious purpose.

Synonyms: consecrated, dedicated, devout, divine, hallowed, humble, just, moral, perfect, pure, revered, righteous, spotless, sublime, uncorrupt, upright, venerable, virtuous.

You must be holy because I, the Lord, am holy. I have set you apart from all other people to be my very own.

—Leviticus 20:26 NLT

One year on a Christmas vacation when I was a child, my family visited Carlsbad Caverns in New Mexico. To my twelve-year-old mind, the underground caves with the stalactites and stalagmites were awesome. On the route to the Big Room, our tour followed steep and narrow trails that descended more than 750 feet underground. It was cold, damp, and dark down there. When everyone arrived at the end of the trail, the lights along the path were turned off. It was the blackest black I have ever seen. A person can take pictures, but a flash doesn't do much to light up the darkness there. After the tour, when we arrived at the surface again, the sunlight was almost blinding.

I don't know whether a person could condition himself to the darkness in the caverns and begin to see anything. We have conditioned ourselves to the darkness around us, though. What used to be sin has become "a little mistake." "Stretching the truth" doesn't sound like telling a lie. We have accustomed ourselves to the darkness around us, and sin doesn't seem all that bad.

God is holy. For most of us, the response is, "Yeah, and I'm not."

I can't help thinking about the relationships in my life that have deteriorated due to my pride and inability to forgive.

But compared to a lot of other people, I'm not doing that bad.

OK, I'm impatient and think more about myself than others.

But there are a lot worse sins that that.

Well, I do have some thoughts I wouldn't want anyone to know about.

But everybody has some of those.

> They are only comparing themselves with each other, and measuring themselves by themselves. What foolishness!
> —2 Corinthians 10:12 NLT

God is our standard for holiness, not other people.

What does this very religious-sounding word mean: "holy"?

It's more than purity. It's more than moral excellence. Holy means "set apart" and "to take a stand." When we say God is holy, we mean he is set apart from sin. As A.W. Tozer puts it, "If he were to tell us how white he is, we would understand it in terms of only dingy gray."[2]

God is our standard for holiness, not other people.

God cannot tolerate or excuse sin—any sin. Sin separates us from God. I hope that's comforting to you and not frightening. We worship a God with a standard *that* perfect and *that* pure.

> "I want God to be what God is: the impeccably holy, the All-Holy One. I want him to be and remain THE HOLY. I want his heaven to be holy and his throne to be holy. I don't want him to change or modify his requirements. Even if it shuts me out, I want something holy left in the universe."[3]
>
> —A.W. Tozer

And because God is holy he wants us to be holy. Then we can have a relationship and not a wall between us. For he himself has said, "You must be holy because I am holy."

—I Peter 1:15-16 NLT

I know how it feels when my children disrespect what I say or don't listen to me. I wonder how God feels when we don't take seriously what he says. Holiness will show in my thoughts and actions, but it has to start in my heart.

> Therefore if any person is [ingrafted] in Christ (the Messiah) he is a new creation (a new creature altogether); the old [previous moral and spiritual condition] has passed away.
> —2 Corinthians 5:17 AMPLIFIED

As a new creation in Christ, I am not perfect, but God sees me that way. That's encouraging while I'm in the difficult process of becoming Christ-like. I am becoming holy by applying a daily dose of God's Word to my mind. Believe and obey it, presto, change-o! I wish holiness came that easily. Little by little, God's Word has a purifying effect on us. We learn to love what is right and hate what is wrong. Now when I fall short of God's standard, I am sensitized to it because the Holy Spirit lives in me. If I have grieved God's heart, I want to make it right immediately.

The problem comes when I rationalize what I'm doing—when I continue to push aside the Holy Spirit's promptings to repent or to take a stand for what is right. And when I don't care that I have unconfessed sin in my heart. Yes, God is kind and merciful, but he is holy and cannot condone sin. A. W. Tozer gives us an additional thought.

"Whatever is holy is healthy; evil is a moral sickness that must end ultimately in death. The formation of the language itself suggests this, the English word *holy* deriving from the Anglo-Saxon *halig, hal*, meaning, 'well, whole.'"[4] Isn't that just like God? Holiness means "wholeness." Do you want to be whole? Be holy!

Holiness is not about abstaining, self-control, and determination as much as it is about loving Jesus.

It's not so much about a set of rules, it's about not wanting to disappoint the one who's most important in my life.

It's about a love relationship with my heavenly Father, who wants me to resemble him in my words and actions and attitudes.

Am I starting to look like my dad?

I Praise You Because You Are Holy!

To read about worshiping our holy God, read Revelation 4.

Questions for Reflection

Have you allowed other people to become your standard for holiness instead of God? In what ways?

Why is God's holiness important?

What personal significance does it have for you?

Evaluate your love for God. Is pleasing him your highest priority?

Pray

Lord, I praise you that you are absolutely pure and holy—and that will never change. I'm thankful you don't compromise your standards. I have become so accustomed to the sin around me it doesn't faze me like it used to. Give me a fresh picture of your holiness through your Spirit. I want to live in wholeness. In your holy name, Amen.

Related Verses

> In a great chorus they sang, "Holy, holy, holy is the Lord Almighty! The whole earth is filled with his glory!"
> —Isaiah 6:2-3 NLT

> The holiness of God is displayed by his righteousness.
> —Isaiah 5:16 NLT

> The nature of your reign, O Lord, is holiness forever.
> —Psalm 93:5 NLT

Chapter 9

GOD IS COMPASSIONATE

God emotionally identifies with your pain, joy, hopes, and dreams, and has chosen to allow your happiness to affect his own.[1]

—Chip Ingram

Compassionate: marked by sympathetic consciousness of others' distress together with a desire to alleviate it.; share the suffering of; implies pity coupled with an urgent desire to aid or to spare.

Synonyms: sympathetic, pitying, understanding.

The LORD is gracious and righteous; our God is full of compassion.

—Psalm 116:5 NIV

It was a day full of dark, ominous clouds and weather warnings. As they drove, my parents were noticing the odd shapes of the storm clouds when suddenly a tornado emerged out of the gray sky. In a moment it was on the ground just a few miles ahead of them. They hadn't planned to be storm chasers that afternoon, but they were the first to arrive at a farmhouse just hit by a tornado. A man needed help and his wife had perished in the disaster. My parents were able to offer help, pray, and stay with them until medical help arrived.

Compassion is your hurt in God's heart. In the storms of your life, God is compassionate. He sees your broken heart and shares your suffering. He's concerned about you.

> You care about the anguish of my soul.
> —Psalm 31:7 NLT

The many miracles Jesus performed are recorded in Matthew, Mark, Luke, and John. He worked miracles for various reasons. Sometimes it was to teach a lesson or as a sign of his identity. Often it was because he felt compassion for the suffering and pain the people were experiencing.

> A vast crowd was there as he stepped from the boat, and he had compassion on them and healed their sick.
> —Matthew 14:14 NLT

It's a little hard to imagine that Almighty God, Creator of the universe, actually feels emotions like I do. He somehow seems above tears and sorrow. Jesus could have said "be healed" from a distance. He could have limited his miracles to stilling the waves, feeding many people, or putting a coin in a fish's mouth.

Instead, Jesus' life story is full of compassionate instances. He touched the leper. He cried with his friends at Lazarus's tomb. He was concerned when someone was hurting physically or emotionally.

> When he saw the crowds, he had compassion on them, because they were harassed and helpless, like sheep without a shepherd.
> —Matthew 9:36 NIV

Jesus called his disciples to him and said, "I have compassion for these people; they have already been with me three days and have nothing to eat. I do not want to send them away hungry, or they may collapse on the way."
—Matthew 15:32 NIV

Jesus had compassion on them and touched their eyes. Immediately they received their sight and followed him.
—Matthew 20:34 NIV

Filled with compassion, Jesus reached out his hand and touched the man. "I am willing," he said. "Be clean!"
—Mark 1:41 NIV

When you are mourning, or if you've been disappointed or rejected, Jesus feels compassion for you. He cares intensely about the situation in your life. Jesus was "moved with compassion" again and again as he healed people, fed them, and touched them. He did more than feel sorry for people. He was actively compassionate.

> When you are mourning, or if you've been disappointed or rejected, Jesus feels compassion for you.

Even Jesus' stories were full of compassion. In Luke 15, he tells about a young man who left home on bad terms with his family. When the son came to his senses and finally returned, the father was filled with compassion for him and, throwing aside protocol, ran to his returning son. Rather than feeling angry or revengeful at the son who had disappointed him, this father was full of loving compassion.

> So he got up and went to his father. "But while he was still a long way off, his father saw him and was filled with compassion for him; he ran to his son, threw his arms around him and kissed him."
>
> —Luke 15:20 NIV

It takes love and concern for others to show them compassion. Don't depend on a self-absorbed person to show compassion. When we allow God to love others through us, we don't look at people the same way. Listen to Lloyd Ogilvie's words.

> "Suddenly, life takes on a new quality. People with needs are not a burden. They are gifts of God for us to give away what he has given us. In the same way, when we are troubled and anxious, we can be sure that someone under orders from the Lord will be deployed in our lives for just the right word of encouragement, correction, or practical help we need."[2]

The more we know of Jesus, the more we want to be like him. As believers, when someone is in need, compassion should become the compelling motivation of the moment.

> You keep track of all my sorrows. You have collected all my tears in your bottle.
>
> —Psalm 56:8 NLT

I Praise You Because You Are Compassionate!

To read about the compassion Jesus showed read Matthew 9 and Mark 5.

Questions for Reflection

Can you recall a time when you felt God's compassion for you?

How does it make you feel to know that God cares when you are hurting?

Imagine a scale of compassion with self-absorbed at one end and Christ's kind of compassion at the other end. Where are you on the scale?

Is there someone who needs your compassion now?

Pray

Lord, it's amazing to me that you care on such a human level for my needs. You care when I'm hurting. When I'm feeling down you not only notice, you're concerned. Help me to develop a compassionate heart so I can show the same kind of compassion to others as you have shown to me. Give me a heart of love so I can be your hands and feet. Amen.

Related Verses

> Once again you will have compassion on us. You will trample our sins under your feet and throw them into the depths of the ocean!
>
> —Micah 7:19 NLT

The Lord is like a father to his children, tender and compassionate to those who fear him.
—Psalm 103:13 NLT

The Lord is gracious and compassionate, slow to anger and rich in love.
—Psalm 145:8 NIV

Chapter 10

God Is Victorious

You will find in thus knowing God as your sovereign protector, irrevocably committed to you in the covenant of grace, both freedom from fear and new strength for the fight.[1]

—J. I. Packer

Victorious: being the winner in a contest or struggle; characteristic of or expressing a sense of victory or fulfillment; defeating of an enemy or opponent; successful in a struggle against difficulties or an obstacle; the state of having triumphed.

Synonyms: triumphant, successful, conquering.

No, despite all these things, overwhelming victory is ours through Christ, who loved us.

—Romans 8:37 NLT

When we were teenagers, my sister and I were part of our church's traveling youth choir. My sister was an alto, but because we needed sopranos our director asked her to switch to the soprano section. One of our songs, "We Are More Than Conquerors," was based on Romans 8:37. At the end of the song the sopranos hit a very high note that my sister consistently hit loud and clear. Our director called her "the alto who tried harder." Years later, my sister and her family endured harsh living conditions as missionaries in northern China. No doubt the words to that song and her attitude in singing them contributed to her overcoming the difficult circumstances there.

Some Christians live like victims instead of conquerors. They live selfishly and without hope. Satan tries to defeat us in many ways. He pushes every button he can find until he finds one to which we respond. What is it for you: discouragement, depression, self-pity, condemnation?

While it's not a sin to be tempted, when we give in to temptation, a vicious cycle begins. There are many sins that cause even Christians to live a defeated life. Dangerous habits that have taken root in us. Wrong mindsets and mental strongholds that keep them trapped. Attitudes that reflect stinking thinking. Lack of passion for God or his Word. Maybe your life situation is causing you to feel hopeless—your finances are a mess, you've received a bad report from the doctor, a family member has deserted you. Whether it's sin or circumstances, you may feel you're facing a battle you can't win. The odds are stacked high against you.

God is victorious! Christ won the victory on the cross, and we can be victorious, too! When we're caught in a spiral of distressing circumstances, we should cry to God to be delivered from them. In Romans 8:37, Paul isn't talking about escape *from* our troubles. He says there is triumph *in* them.

> Christ won the victory on the cross, and we can be victorious, too!

> *Despite all these things* (NLT) we can make it!
> *Amid all these things* (Amplified) God is still with us!
> *In all these things* (NIV) God is in control!

Then comes the best part. The presence and power of Christ make it possible for us to triumph to such an extent that the word Paul uses for it is used only once in Scripture. It means we are super-conquerors.

> We are *more than conquerors* NIV
> We *overwhelmingly conquer* NASB
> *Overwhelming victory is ours* NLT
> *We have won more than a victory* CEV

A win is enough, but God has promised us even more than that. What comfort! What peace! What courage and confidence we can have knowing that God is going to see us through our problems!

On the night before Jesus went to the cross, he carefully instructed his disciples on some important matters. In John 16:33 he summed up all he was teaching.

> I have told you all this so that you may have peace in me. Here on earth you will have many trials and sorrows. But take heart, because I have overcome the world.
> —John 16:33 NLT

We will have struggles because this world is a battleground. The battle appeared to be turning in Satan's direction when Jesus hung on the cross. It looked like Satan would be victorious. Apparent defeat changed to victory when Jesus rose from the dead. Christ conquered death and we need not fear death or evil.

> For every child of God defeats this evil world by trusting Christ to give the victory. And the ones who win this battle against the world are the ones who believe that Jesus is the Son of God.
> —I John 5:4-5 NLT

Those who are halfhearted in their obedience to Christ never expect victory because they have lost sight of the victory that is ours through Christ. Instead of giving up, admit you need God's help. Trust in his Word and not in your feelings. Remember that no opposition can crush you. God's Spirit in you is greater than the spirit of the world. The power that brought Jesus back to life is available to you—power for victory over sins that hinder your progress, and power for victory over circumstances that discourage you.

As we move from victory to victory, we grow stronger in our relationship with Christ. So let the battle rage around us—we are *more than* conquerors!

> Don't be afraid, for I am with you. Do not be dismayed, for I am your God. I will strengthen you. I will help you. I will uphold you with my victorious right hand.
> —Isaiah 41:10 NLT

I Praise You Because You Are Victorious!

Read 2 Chronicles 20 for a story of God bringing a dynamic victory.

Questions for Reflection

Are you living like a victim or a conqueror? In what ways?

Is there a situation from which you've been praying to be delivered when perhaps instead God wants to give you victory by going through it?

On the cross Jesus conquered death and sin. What does that mean for you?

Read in Ephesians 6 about the weapons God has given us. How will you use them to be victorious?

Pray

Almighty God, I am no match for what life throws at me. My trust is in you and your Word. Life's pressures will not discourage me, because you are on my side. You are more than enough for any problem I may face. Thank you for winning the victory so that I too can be victorious! In the name of Jesus, Amen.

Related Verses

All who are victorious will inherit all these blessings, and I will be their God, and they will be my children.
—Revelation 21:7 NLT

No weapon formed against you shall prosper, and every tongue which rises against you in judgment you shall condemn. This is the heritage of the servants of the LORD, and their righteousness is from me," says the LORD.

—Isaiah 54:17 NKJV

Some nations boast of their armies and weapons, but we boast in the Lord our God.

—Psalm 20:7 NLT

Chapter 11

GOD IS JUST

The character of God is the guarantee that all wrongs will be righted someday.[1]

—J. I. Packer

Just: having a basis in or conforming to fact or reason; conforming to a standard of correctness; morally right or good.

Synonyms: fair, upright, honest.

He will judge the world with justice and rule the nations with fairness. The Lord is known for his justice.

—Psalm 9:8, 16 NLT

It's not fair—he got new shoes and I didn't!"
"Her piece of candy is bigger than mine!"
Even as children, life sometimes seems unfair. As we grow older the situations change, but our desire for justice does not. Justice is a natural desire in every one of us. When we are treated unfairly we want to take action. We want revenge.

Steve took his wedding vows and meant it when he said, "Til death do us part." The marriage produced three sons. Then his wife suffered mental problems and the marriage ended. Steve gained custody of his boys, only to have his ex-wife kidnap them. Steve was cautious when he started dating again. He took his time, prayed for guidance, and sought counsel from his pastor. He married a second time and things were looking up—until one day he came home from work to an empty house. During the day his wife had loaded all their belongings and moved out. She'd abandoned him.

It wasn't fair! Steve did not deserve what life had handed him. The good news is that Steve trusted in God's justice. Today he is happily married, and his sons are grown and serving the Lord. We, too, may be lied about, misunderstood, or ripped off. Maybe you didn't deserve the treatment you received. Sometimes we become impatient with God to make things right, and we become discouraged. If we do not trust God to vindicate us, we will be susceptible to bitterness and self-pity. If we lose sight of the fact that God is just, we may feel angry, cheated, betrayed, or deceived.

Many of the Psalms deal with this theme. In Psalm 35, David was crying out for justice! He was hunted down and falsely accused, so David cried to God because of his unfair treatment. Then he gave the matter to God, asking him to come to his defense.

Jesus' disciples also wanted justice. Jesus asked them to go ahead of him to a Samaritan village and prepare for his arrival there. When the people in the village rejected Jesus, the disciples asked him if they should call down fire from heaven on them (Luke 9:51-55).

Because people's actions are unjust, we sometimes think God is like that, too. But God is always just. He is the standard for justice. Because of that, everything he does is fair, whether we understand it or not.

God's attributes never quarrel with one another because God is unitary. This means God is not made up of different parts that work in harmony. He is simply one. We are not made like that. For instance, we feel troubled when we are caught between feeling mercy and justice toward a person. Everything God does harmonizes with everything else he does. There is no conflict between God's justice and his mercy.

How could a loving God send a person to hell? Many people believe God is loving but not just. Because his attributes are never in conflict, God's love and justice do not conflict. When God's justice is applied to an unrepentant sinner, justice condemns him to death. When God's justice is applied to a sinner saved by grace, justice sentences him to live. God's justice is consistent in both cases. Each person is receiving what he deserves. God cannot be loving without being just. Even our human laws tell us that wrong needs to be punished. When God punishes sin or forgives sin, both actions are completely consistent with who he is.

The Greek word for just, *dikaios,* means the perfect agreement between God's nature and his acts. God is morally equal, or just. We are morally unequal, or unjust. Because God is just, I can be forgiven of my moral "unequalness," my sin, and live in heaven forever. The fact that God is just means he sees the injustices in our lives.

You tried to help someone and he or she took advantage of you. Someone you trusted did not keep his or her vows to you. You gave your best, yet you were betrayed. Give up the vengeful thoughts. Put down your sword. In God's wisdom and sovereignty he will mete out justice. Vengeance is in God's hands. We can trust him to be true to his character and bring about a just resolution.

God has supreme authority. The Bible tells us that he alone is the judge. God sees the heart, so we must rest in God's justice. He sees what has happened. He knows all about it. Leave it with him.

God sees the heart, so we must rest in God's justice.

> Just and true are your ways, O king of the nations.
> —Revelation 15:3 NLT

I Praise You Because You Are Just!

Read Romans 1 and 2 to understand more about God's justice.

Questions for Reflection

Recall a situation you felt was unfair. How did you handle it?

Read Psalm 17 or Psalm 35. How did David handle injustice?

Describe how God's goodness is part of his justice.

What unfair situation do you need to place in God's hands?

Pray

Dear God, you are just and fair in all you do. You see people's motives and intentions when all I see is their outward actions. Forgive me for becoming impatient and discouraged when I look at the unfairness all around me. Although I do not understand your ways, I trust your character. Thank you that you will make all things right one day. In your name, Amen.

Related Verses

He is the Rock; his work is perfect. Everything he does is just and fair. He is a faithful God who does no wrong; how just and upright he is!
—Deuteronomy 32:4 NLT

For you have upheld my right and my cause; you have sat on your throne, judging righteously.
—Psalm 9:4 NIV

I am storing up these things, sealing them away within my treasury. I will take vengeance; I will repay those who deserve it. In due time their feet will slip. Their day of disaster will arrive, and their destiny will overtake them.
—Deuteronomy 32:34-35 NLT

Chapter 12

GOD IS TRUSTWORTHY

> If we have been learning to worship God and to trust him, the crisis will reveal that we will go to the breaking point and not break in our confidence in him.[1]
> —Oswald Chambers

Trustworthy: warranting trust; reliable.

Synonyms: authentic, believable, credible, ethical, reliable, valid.

We usually hesitate to trust someone we don't know very well. You may have had the experience of trusting someone too soon, then the truth came out after you'd trusted the person with your heart or your money.

Knowing and loving God is our greatest privilege. The better we know him, the more we trust him.

> Those who know your name trust in you. For you, O Lord, have never abandoned anyone who searches for you.
> —Psalm 9:10 NLT

The Amplified Bible uses the words *lean on* and *confidently rely on* for trust. Part of trusting is having a tolerance for uncertainty. Most of us don't like an unknown, uncertain future. We want to know when, where, how—we want control! But guess what? An uncertain future is characteristic of life! The only way to deal with that is to trust the one who does know the future.

The tiny rowboat my husband and I rode in was loaded heavily with provisions for our Canadian fishing trip. Our boat was so full I couldn't see my husband's head over the supplies. Ten family members, three boats and one huge lake!

We anxiously searched for the lone stretch of sandy beach on the lake. Each inlet we passed held trees growing up to the water's edge, making it impossible to set up camp. As the sun set, we prayed. We clung to the fact that my father had been to this beach before. At dusk finally came the welcome, sandy sight!

I have grown to trust God more as I've come to know him better. The promises in God's Word tell us he is trustworthy, but sometimes we have to learn it by experience. Those experiences build on one another to create a strong bond of trust.

Believing God's Word gives me confidence in his character, which grows my faith, which calms my fears. The promises in God's Word are an ideal way to test his trustworthiness. If someone says he or she is going to do something and then does it—again and again—I trust that person. God says:

- No weapon formed against you will prosper. Isaiah 54:17 KJV
- If God is for us, who can be against us? Romans 8:31 KJV
- No good thing will he withhold from them who do what is right. Psalm 84:11 NLT
- When the enemy comes in like a flood, the Spirit of God will lift up a standard again him. Isaiah 59:19 KJV
- He will not allow any temptation that is more than we can bear. I Corinthians 10:13 KJV
- He is able to accomplish more than we would ever dare to ask or hope. Ephesians 3:20 NLT

>
> The promises in God's Word tell us he is trustworthy, but sometimes we have to learn it by experience.
>

- He has plans for good for us, to give us a future and a hope. Jeremiah 29:11 NLT

I can truly say God has never failed me—but he has scared me to death a few times! I've experienced his faithfulness. I know he will protect, provide, make a way, figure it out. We sometimes find it easier to trust God when we're in a bind: we've tried everything else—now we might as well pray! When life is going smoothly, we're tempted to trust ourselves. If we rely on ourselves, our trust in God will atrophy. We must exercise our trust in God even when it seems frightening to do so.

People will let us down, too. They sometimes prove untrustworthy. If that has happened to you, give God a try. You won't be disappointed. He's a perfect parent. An ideal friend.

If you've ever gone to sleep only to wake a few hours later and have your mind tumbling and tumbling with worries, I have a solution. God's Word says, "You will keep in perfect peace all who trust in you, whose thoughts are fixed on you!" (Isaiah 26:3 NLT)

I repeat this verse to myself. I focus my thoughts and fix my mind on God, whom I trust. It never fails! I'm off to sleep!

Your Father has already been where you are and is there now. He is trustworthy.

I Praise You Because You Are Trustworthy!

For further study, read David's words of trust in Psalm 31.

Questions for Reflection

Is there someone you trusted before you knew him or her well? Did you find him or her trustworthy?

Do you find it difficult to give God control of your life? What is at the root of your wanting control?

Record an incident in which God proved himself trustworthy to you.

With what do you need to trust God at this time?

Pray

Lord, I admit it's scary to trust you sometimes. Even though my trust may be weak, I realize it's better than relying on myself. Whatever is ahead of me, I know you're already there. I choose to trust you. Amen.

Related Verses

> You heard their cries for help and saved them. They put their trust in you and were never disappointed.
> —Psalm 22:5 NLT

> No one who trusts in you will ever be disgraced.
> —Psalm 25:3 NLT

> The Lord is my strength, my shield from every danger. I trust him with all my heart.
> —Psalm 28:7 NLT

Chapter 13

God Is Merciful

Forever his mercy stands, a boundless, overwhelming immensity of divine pity and compassion.[1]
—A.W. Tozer

Merciful: full of mercy—mercy is compassion or forbearance shown to an offender or subject; a blessing that is an act of divine favor or compassion; implies compassion that forbears punishing even when justice demands it.

Synonyms: compassionate, sympathetic, gracious, beneficent.

He saved us, not because of the good things we did, but because of his mercy. He washed away our sins and gave us a new life through the Holy Spirit.
—Titus 3:5 NLT

I was sixteen and had just received my driver's license. My summer job was waiting tables at a small diner about three miles from home, and I worked the early morning shift. My mom decided to let me drive her car to work since I would be home shortly after noon. I appreciated my parents' trust in me, so I tried hard to be careful. But one day as I was backing out of the tiny parking lot at the small diner, I backed into a Pepsi truck and put a dent in the rear passenger door. I cried and was scared because the car, a 1967 Chevrolet Caprice, was the first new car my dad had ever owned. I didn't know what the punishment for my carelessness would be. When I got home and gave my parents the awful news, they showed me mercy. I know my dad felt bad and they knew I felt terrible.

We choose on a daily basis how we will respond to people's transgressions. We can ignore them, remain aloof, harden our hearts, or show mercy.

All of us need mercy. We have all sinned and, without God's mercy, we're doomed. Mercy is God's compassion, his kindness towards us. Mercy and compassion are similar in definition and sometimes used interchangeably. Compassion, though, is sympathy with a person's distress and a desire to alleviate it. Mercy is compassion shown to an *offender*.

Did you walk in the flesh this week? Did you follow your own desires? Did you ignore God's voice or displease him in some way? Then you offended God and earned his judgment. Instead, he offers his mercy.

> It is of the Lord's mercies that we are not consumed, because his compassions fail not.
> —Lamentations 3:22 KJV

Mercy is also defined as "the giving of a second chance"—even when we don't deserve it. Did anyone ever give you a second chance? Maybe you flunked out, failed the test, fell miserably, flubbed up, or forgot something important. When someone gives you another chance, it's because he or she believes in you. God believes in you—he's full of second chances! Our mistakes and sins will never use up God's mercy because God doesn't stock a supply of mercy. Mercy is just who God is.

God's mercy doesn't go into action only when we ask for it or need it. God's mercy is there all the time—bending down to help us, withholding judgment. A.W. Tozer said, "We get the odd notion that God is showing mercy because Jesus died. No—Jesus died because God is showing mercy. It was the mercy of God that gave us Calvary, not Calvary that gave us mercy."[2]

Mercy won't let go of us. Even in the most sinful heart, God's mercy is at work. When God's justice confronts our sin, the sentence is death. Mercy postpones that.

God's mercy is there all the time—bending down to help us, withholding judgment.

God isn't stingy with his mercy. The Bible tells us that he is full of mercy (James 5:11). It also says God's mercy reaches to the heavens (Psalm 57:10), is abundant (Psalm 86:5), is from everlasting to everlasting (Psalm 103:17), is very great (I Chronicles 21:13), is tender (Psalm 69:16), is plentiful (Psalm 69:16), and endures forever (Psalm 136:2).

I find it interesting that nearly half the references to mercy in the Bible are found in the book of Psalms. King David was a man of God. Could part of the reason for that be because he was well acquainted with God's mercy? He hoped in it, was confident in it, asked for it, rejoiced in it, and sang about it.

Tozer says, "Mercy is God's goodness confronting human guilt and suffering."[3] Whatever our need is determines which of God's attributes we'll celebrate at this moment.

Doesn't that make you want to throw a party and praise God for his mercy?

By the way, that same summer, I dented my parents' car two more times. I learned a lot about mercy!

> The unfailing love of the Lord never ends! By his mercies we have been kept from complete destruction. Great is his faithfulness, his mercies begin afresh each day.
> —Lamentations 3:22-23 NLT

I Praise You Because You Are Merciful!

To read more about God's mercy, read Psalm 136.

Questions for Reflection

Can you think of a time when God in his mercy gave you a second chance?

What is your response to God for the mercy he has shown you?

In light of God's mercy to you, what will your response be to others?

We who have received mercy must show mercy. How will you show mercy today?

Pray

God, I am thankful that your mercies are new every morning. I am grateful that your mercies are plentiful and tender. You give your mercy for my failings over and over again. Help me not to take it for granted. When others disappoint and fail me, help me to be merciful towards them as you are to me. In Jesus' name, Amen.

Related Verses

> The LORD has already told you what is good, and this is what he requires: to do what is right, to love mercy, and to walk humbly with your God.
> —Micah 6:8 NLT

> With everlasting kindness will I have mercy on thee, saith the Lord thy Redeemer.
> —Isaiah 54:8 KJV

> Once you were not a people; now you are the people of God. Once you received none of God's mercy; now you have received his mercy.
> —I Peter 2:10 NLT

Chapter 14

GOD IS ETERNAL

For him time does not pass, it remains.[1]

—A.W. Tozer

Eternal: being without beginning or end; existing outside of time; continuing without interruption; perpetual; forever true or changeless.

Synonyms: infinite, timeless, endless, everlasting.

Lord, you have been our dwelling place throughout all generations. Before the mountains were born or you brought forth the earth and the world, from everlasting to everlasting you are God.

—Psalm 90:1-2 NIV

We live in a time-bound world. We live with schedules and deadlines. There are moments when we wish time would pass more quickly and there are times when the days seem to drag on and on. Waiting for Christmas to arrive, the days are filled with excitement and anticipation. When we're on vacation time seems to fly by. Then there are times in life when our schedules are interrupted. Time stands still for us while we grieve, endure an illness, or recover from divorce. Time is our friend and time is our enemy.

God is eternal! Time does not apply to God. It is not a concern with God. He has always existed and will always exist. He has no beginning and no end.

God is outside of time. He doesn't work on our timetable.

> But you must not forget, dear friends, that a day is like a thousand years to the Lord, and a thousand years is like a day.
> —II Peter 3:8 NLT

Our minds are bound up in the here and now. The immediate occupies our minds. *What will I make for dinner tonight? When will I have time to finish the laundry?* It is even hard to save money for retirement because it seems so far away. We worry about trivial things. We hurry about, doing unimportant things.

The choices we make today have impact in eternity. The habits, the attitudes, the lifestyles we choose determine whom we become. It's easy to allow the immediate things to overtake the important things in our lives. Life is too short to be critical. With God's help we can learn to see beyond the immediate and live with an eternal perspective. The way we live our lives will affect generations to follow us.

> Teach us to make the most of our time, so that we may grow in wisdom.
> —Psalm 90:12 NLT

God is eternal and his Word is eternal.

> The grass withers, and the flowers fade but the word of our God stands forever.
> —Isaiah 40:8 NLT

His blessings are eternal.

> For when you grant a blessing, O Lord, it is an eternal blessing!
> —I Chronicles 17:27 NLT

Even though we have a limited amount of time on earth, we, too, are eternal beings. We will spend eternity with God or without him. This should change our perspective on our circumstances and our relationships. We worry about horizontal things and pay little attention to the vertical.

God sees our lives from an eternal perspective. He sees us from conception all the way through our journey on earth. When we're frustrated or annoyed, we need to ask ourselves if these situations are of eternal importance. When we become so focused on the here and now, it's easy to get bent out of shape. We would do well to ask ourselves whether a situation is of eternal consequence and what difference it might make in the light of eternity. God sees the big picture and knows the implications of each event.

God's Word stands forever. His promises stand

As we learn to see our lives from an eternal standpoint, our priorities and values will begin to change.

forever. He has made us eternal beings. As we learn to see our lives from an eternal standpoint, our priorities and values will begin to change. The little frustrations of life will become just that—little.

Has life here on earth been so great that you don't want to leave? No matter how wonderful our lives on earth, we never will be completely satisfied with life here because God has planted eternity in our hearts. We have eternal value. Our lives have meaning both now and for eternity. Set aside the things that don't really matter. Material things only bring temporary happiness. One day we will each leave this existence and be born into eternity, and time for us will be no more.

> God has made everything beautiful for its own time. He has planted eternity in the human heart, but even so, people cannot see the whole scope of God's work from beginning to end.
> —Ecclesiastes 3:11 NLT

I Praise You Because You Are Eternal!

For more reading on eternity, read Psalm 102.

Questions for Reflection

Is time passing too quickly or too slowly for you now? Why?

What temporal issues are you allowing to surpass the eternal ones?

What choices are you making today that will last for eternity?

Why should we praise God for being eternal?

Pray

Everlasting Father, I want my life to count for eternity. Whatever my days bring, staying at home with my children, working outside my home, driving in the carpool, I want my days to count. I want to live in such a way that trivial matters do not consume me. Raise my eyes to what will count for eternity. Establish the work of my hands. For your glory, Amen.

Related Verses

In ages past you laid the foundation of the earth, and the heavens are the work of your hands. Even they will perish, but you remain forever; they will wear out like old clothing. You will change them like a garment, and they will fade away. But you are always the same; your years never end.
—Psalm 102:25-27 NLT

He existed before everything else began, and he holds all creation together.
—Colossians 1:17 NLT

God replied, "I am the one who always is."
—Exodus 3:14 NLT

Chapter 15

GOD IS SOVEREIGN

> Only a sovereign Lord can orchestrate all the instruments that are playing in our lives to produce music of hope and significance.[1]
> —Cynthia Heald

> Sovereign: self-governing; independent; having supreme rank or power; paramount; supreme.

> Synonyms: absolute, autonomous, chief, highest, independent, kingly, predominant, supreme, unlimited.

> For I am God—I alone! I am God, and there is no one else like me. Only I can tell you what is going to happen even before it happens. Everything I plan will come to pass, for I do whatever I wish.
> —Isaiah 46:10 NLT

We are all answerable to someone—our bosses, for starters.

If you are married, you and your spouse are accountable to each other.

But maybe you're a self-employed single person!

All that needs to be said, then, is this: April 15. That reminds us we're answerable to Uncle Sam—at least for how much money we make. Checks and balances bind even the president of the United States, who has tremendous authority.

There is only one who is answerable only to himself: God. He is sovereign. I love that word. It sounds so regal and mighty. And it is.

> "I am God," he tells us, " and there is no one else like me. Only I can tell you what is going to happen even before it happens. Everything I plan will come to pass, for I do whatever I wish."
>
> —Isaiah 46:9-10 NLT

The dictionary defines sovereign as "governing from a position of superlative strength and efficiency. Supreme in authority. To rule in complete independence."

God governs everything without any outside influence. He's in charge! He has absolute freedom to do what he wills to do. God doesn't play by ear or doodle. He is intentional and purposeful in all he does.

There are times when certain acts of God, including his choices in our lives, don't seem consistent with his character. We may question why things happen. We may even question God's love or his goodness.

After a difficult situation several years ago, I had a lot of questions. I became quite tormented with the thoughts of why a good God would allow so much pain. It was then I came upon Proverbs 20:24: "Since the Lord is directing our steps, why try to understand everything that happens along the way?" (TLB).

When we get caught up in asking God why, we become like a three-year-old asking a parent why over and over. If you're a parent and your children ask for Oreos for breakfast, you know that you have more information about healthful eating than they do. You're seeing their situation from a different perspective. They don't understand it the way you do—and they can't. They don't have the capabilities. And some things they just don't need to know!

We see things from a very limited perspective. God sees and controls the big picture. He engineers circumstances. What a great description of what God is doing—he manages, arranges, and directs our lives perfectly. Our present situation is part of God's whole plan. At times we wonder if the events of our lives are really a part of his plan or if he has forgotten about us. That is when God is asking us to trust him even though we can't see what he is doing.

I've heard it said that "God's will is exactly what you and I would choose if we knew what God knows." While some people might be afraid of someone who has this kind of authority, I find tremendous security in his sovereignty because God's love conditions everything he does. He loves me—and he's in charge!

For all you other inquiring minds who just want to know, keep this in mind: There is something more important than understanding—and that is trusting. I might not understand why it happened, but God does. Some things will remain a mystery to us until we get to heaven.

> For as the heavens are higher than the earth, so are my ways higher than your ways and my thoughts than your thoughts.
> —Isaiah 55:8 KJV

When we have given our lives to Christ, we have absolutely nothing to fear. He is in charge. Even when life isn't working out the way you want, will you trust that God knows what he is doing? He never makes a mistake. He will even take our mistakes and miraculously turn them into something he can use—if we will trust him. He is in complete control of this universe and your situation.

>
> Even when life isn't working out the way you want, will you trust that God knows what he is doing?
>

I Praise You Because You Are Sovereign!

For further reading on God's sovereignty, read Hannah's prayer in I Samuel 2:1-10.

Questions for Reflection

To whom are you accountable?

If your friend was questioning why God allows certain hard things to happen, what would you tell him or her?

Is there an area of your life in which it is hard to accept God's sovereignty?

When you truly believe God is sovereign, what will be the result in your life?

Pray

Sovereign God, I have many questions. The situations that didn't turn out like I thought they would or should sometimes make me wonder where you are. Help me to remember that you are in control, governing all according to your good purposes. It gives me peace, joy, and hope when I recognize your supreme authority. I trust you. In Jesus' name, Amen.

Related Verses

> The Lord does whatever pleases him throughout all heaven and earth and on the seas and in their depths.
> —Psalm 135:6 NLT

> All the people of the earth are nothing compared to him. He has the power to do as he pleases among the angels of heaven and with those who live on earth. No one can stop him or challenge him, saying, "What do you mean by doing these things?"
> —Daniel 4:35 NLT

> He directs the snow to fall on the earth and tells the rain to pour down. Everyone stops working at such a time so they can recognize his power. The wild animals hide in the rocks or in their dens. The stormy wind comes from its chamber, and the driving winds bring the cold. God's breath sends the ice, freezing wide expanses of water. He loads the clouds with moisture, and they flash with his lightning. The clouds turn around and around under his direction. They do whatever he commands throughout the earth. He causes things to happen on earth, either as a punishment or as a sign of his unfailing love.
> —Job 37:6-13 NLT

> Who has done such mighty deeds, directing the affairs of the human race as each new generation marches by? It is I, the Lord, the First and the Last. I alone am he.
> —Isaiah 41:4 NLT

Chapter 16

God Is Relational

For some unfathomable reason, he wants me as his friend, and desires to be my friend, and has given his Son to die for me in order to realize this purpose.[1]

—J. I. Packer

Relational: warmhearted; amicable; enjoying companionship; friend-maker.

Synonyms: bonding, communicative, connecting, friendly near, relevant.

You must worship no other gods, but only the Lord, for he is a God who is passionate about his relationship with you.

—Exodus 34:14 NLT

When you reach into your mailbox and sort through your daily mail, what do you open first? The letters addressed to "Occupant" or "The Household at..." hit the wastebasket first. The envelopes obviously being delivered to the masses don't pique my interest. The letters with a handwritten address or those marked "personal" feel the slice of the letter opener first!

Dale Carnegie says the most important word in the English language is a person's own name. We all like to hear our names. Go ahead, say your name out loud.

God knows you by name—not as a number, not as one of the crowd, but personally. In Exodus, God is talking to Moses. He's saying this to you as well: "I will do the very thing you have asked, because I am pleased with you and I know you by name" (Exodus 33:17 NLT).

When we ask someone his or her name, that's often the starting point for the beginning of a relationship. God is relational.

After meeting a person, we say we know him or her personally. Beyond that is another dimension—having an ongoing relationship with that person. To meet the President of the United States would be wonderful, but to have a day-to-day relationship with him would be an entirely different matter. When you accept Jesus Christ as Savior, a personal relationship with him has begun. Meeting him is only the beginning, though.

There is so much more to knowing God through Jesus than the initial introduction: the ongoing relationship, time spent together, talking, listening, learning about him, and becoming more like him. When we speak to him, he listens. He longs to speak to us.

Some people keep their distance in a relationship. They might be afraid people will see something they don't like. Or they like their space. God, however, pursues an intimate relationship with each of us.

Think of one of your good friends. You spend time together, and listen to each other. You would drop what you're doing to help your friend—day or night. You encourage each other. We tell our children to be careful in their choice of friends because friends have a great influence on us.

God is everything you dream of in a close friend. He listens. He is there for you in hard times. He understands you. He will never leave you. He accepts you as you are. You can trust him. He treats you with respect. He values you. He loves time with you. He loves talking and listening to you.

By knowing you intimately, God knows how to comfort you. He is close to you when you're brokenhearted. You're his treasured child and he is your greatest encourager.

If you haven't met Christ personally, take a moment to talk to him now. Tell him you want a personal relationship with him. In the Garden of Eden, "the Lord God called out to Adam, 'Where are you?'" (Genesis 3:9 NLT). God wanted to spend time with Adam but sin had broken their close relationship. Tell God you're sorry for the things you've done that have hurt him. Perhaps your relationship with him needs to be reconnected or recharged. God actively pursues a close relationship with you.

Honoring God with our lives grows our friendship with him. "Friendship with the Lord is reserved for those who fear him. With them he shares the secrets of his covenant" (Psalm 25:14 NLT). We will live in a way that shows honor to a person whose relationship is important to us. When we honor God, our friendship becomes more intimate and he can confide in us.

One parenting principle that made a big impact on me when my children were

> Honoring God with our lives grows our friendship with him.

young was "rules without relationship equals rebellion." Some parents lay out house rules without really spending time with their children, listening to them, building memories, or having fun together.

Think about it from a child's viewpoint: You're just going to tell me what to do, but you don't really care about me. Our heavenly Father is the perfect parent. He wants a close personal relationship with us. He's not distant, uninterested, or impersonal.

God is passionate about his relationship with you. He offers his forever friendship. Will you accept?

I Praise You Because You Are Relational!

Read about the close relationship between God and Moses in Exodus 33 and 34.

Questions for Reflection

What are some of the qualities you value in a friend?

What are some of the necessary ingredients in a quality relationship?

Have you taken the initial step to having a personal relationship with Jesus Christ? Describe.

How could you move to the next level in your relationship with Christ?

Pray

Lord God, what a privilege it is to be called your friend. Thank you for listening to me, understanding me, and always thinking about me. I treasure my time spent with you. No other relationship can compare with the one I have with you. Amen.

Related Verses

> My heart has heard you say, "Come and talk with me." And my heart responds, "Lord, I am coming."
> —Psalm 27:8 NLT

> I'm no longer calling you servants because servants don't understand what their master is thinking and planning. No, I've named you friends because I've let you in on everything I've heard from the Father.
> —John 15:15 MESSAGE

> God sent him to buy freedom for us who were slaves to the law, so that he could adopt us as his very own children.
> —Galatians 4:5 NLT

Chapter 17

GOD IS ALL-WISE

All God's acts are done in perfect wisdom, first for his own glory, and then for the highest good of the greatest number for the longest time.[1]

—A.W. Tozer

All: being the utmost possible.

Wise: having the ability to discern or judge what is true, right, or lasting; sagacious; having insight; exhibiting common sense; prudent.

Synonyms: completely discerning, perfectly insightful, totally sagacious.

For God is so wise and so mighty. Who has ever challenged him successfully? But true wisdom and power are with God; counsel and understanding are his.

—Job 9:4; 12:13 NLT

In school I was a quiet student. I didn't want to incur the wrath of my teachers, so I didn't talk out of turn during class. I did my homework faithfully and ended up with good grades. In high school, even though my report card looked good, I felt I was coming up short in the common sense department—like the time I asked my driver education teacher how many miles over the speed limit I could go without getting ticketed. To be sure, some of that lack of common sense works itself out in experience. I began to realize that there are different kinds of intelligence—book smarts, emotional intelligence, and social wisdom. Intelligence is measured in lots of different ways from IQ tests to college entrance exams to aptitude tests. It's one thing to memorize some facts, it's quite another to apply those facts to life. In our information age, there is plenty of knowledge, but wisdom is scarce.

God is all-wise. He is also omniscient. What is the difference between these two words? A.W. Tozer helps us understand:

> "The English language, you will notice, has succeeded in creating new words by uniting one word to another. For instance, we take the word *science*, meaning 'knowledge,' and we unite it to the word *omni*, meaning 'all' to create omniscience. But when we come to the word *wisdom*, the word-makers never got around to making such a word. We haven't any such word as 'omniwisdom.'" [2]

God knows and understands everything—he is omniscient. Another facet of God's character is that he is wise. And because he is God, he can't be partly anything. He is infinitely and entirely wise. Otherwise he wouldn't be God.

Like Job's friends, there are people who think they are fountains of wisdom and must spread their wisdom to everyone with whom they come in contact. A rule of thumb in dealing with know-it-alls: do not try to win an argument with them. It may help to feel sorry for them. Just think of the difficulty in being a person who thinks he or she knows it all and must have an argument to answer every statement and an opposing opinion on each issue!

> Oh, what a wonderful God we have! How great are his riches and wisdom and knowledge! How impossible it is for us to understand his decisions and his methods! For who can know what the Lord is thinking? Who knows enough to be his counselor?
>
> —Romans 11:33-34 NLT

God always acts with exact precision in perfect timing. His wisdom is complete and perfect. He sees the past and the future and knows what is best for us. Watch a colony of ants busily working. They are on the move—carrying, building, cooperating. Our view of their activities is much different than what the ant sees. God sees the big picture in our lives. He sees our past, understands our present circumstances, and knows our future. A. W. Tozer states it beautifully.

"He always does what he does with flawless precision, seeing the end from the beginning, never making any mistakes and never asking anything from you that you can't do or don't have. He never makes any unfair demands, but knows you're flesh and treats you with a heart of compassion. Whatever he commands, he gives you the power to obey the command—always. You can trust this kind of God. The difficulty with us is, we don't trust God. And that's why we're in the fix we're in." [3]

There is no way for us to make decisions based on our wisdom alone. We have to make sure we are depending on God's wisdom.

> There is a path before each person that seems right, but it ends in death.
>
> —Proverbs 14:12 NLT

God's Word is the source of all true wisdom. If our actions contradict his Word, we're not only acting unwisely, we're not trusting God. When something looks right to us, we can rationalize it or explain away any argument that would contradict our viewpoint. When God's Word tells us otherwise, the question remains: Whose wisdom are you following, God's or yours? Who is making the final decision—God or you?

> Trust in the Lord with all your heart; do not depend on your own understanding.
> —Proverbs 3:5 NLT

> If our actions contradict his Word, we're not only acting unwisely, we're not trusting God.

We may think we are wise but we desperately need the guidance and stability God gives us. Thankfully, he is happy to give us the wisdom we need for every situation we face.

> If you need wisdom—if you want to know what God wants you to do—ask him, and he will gladly tell you. He will not resent your asking.
> —James 1:5 NLT

I Praise You Because You Are All-wise!

For more on God's wisdom, read Job 38-41.

Questions for Reflection

Have you known someone who had a good amount of knowledge but not much wisdom?

Can you think of a time when you relied on your own wisdom and you knew it was not what God wanted? What was the outcome?

What does depending on God's wisdom mean in your life?

What is he telling you about the decisions you're facing?

Pray

All-wise God, I praise your infinite wisdom. What a privilege it is to be loved by you, knowing that you never make mistakes. I can rely on your understanding of my situation and trust you with control of my life. What security and peace I have because of your wisdom. In Jesus' name, Amen.

Related Verses

> But God made the earth by his power, and he preserves it by his wisdom. He has stretched out the heavens by his understanding.
> —Jeremiah 10:12 NLT

> But do people know where to find wisdom? Where can they find understanding? For it is hidden from the eyes of all humanity. Even the sharp-eyed birds in the sky cannot discover it. But Destruction and Death say, "We

have heard a rumor of where wisdom can be found." God surely knows where it can be found, for he looks throughout the whole earth, under all the heavens. He made the winds blow and determined how much rain should fall. He made the laws of the rain and prepared a path for the lightning. Then, when he had done all this, he saw wisdom and measured it. He established it and examined it thoroughly. And this is what he says to all humanity: "The fear of the Lord is true wisdom; to forsake evil is real understanding."

—Job 28:20-28 NLT

Chapter 18

GOD IS GOOD

The cause of his goodness is in himself; the recipients of his goodness are all his beneficiaries without merit and without recompense.[1]

—A.W. Tozer

Good: of moral excellence; upright; of or possessing a favorable character or nature; that which is comely, agreeable, pleasant and whole.

Synonyms: commendable, virtuous, just, kind.

You are good and do only good.

—Psalm 119:68 NLT

One day when I was in second grade my teacher asked us to answer some questions on paper. One question was "Do you think you do good work?" I was a straight A student in those days, yet I answered "no." Go ahead and analyze me. I don't know what my crazy reason was for thinking that at seven years old. I did excellent work, but perhaps any score of less than 100 percent haunted me. Good and perfect seem to go together in my mind. I knew I made mistakes.

The dictionary lists no less than eighteen definitions for the word *good*. Good is one of those words that can really confuse a person trying to learn the English language. We talk about good news, having good taste, a good book, good looks, a good laugh, a good night's rest. Just what do we mean when we say God is good?

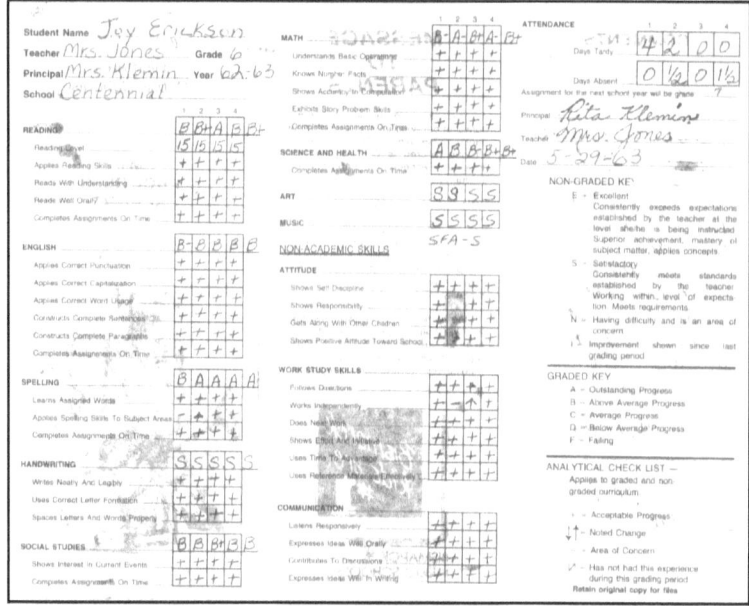

When the Bible says God is good, the writers are saying he is gracious, generous, good-natured, kindhearted, benevolent, and loving. If we described a person like this, he would be nearly perfect. At some funerals you would think the deceased was nearly perfect. Family members say they never heard him speak an unkind word about anyone all his life. They just never *heard* him speak it. No one is like that all the time—except God. He is always good.

Often the phrase "God is good!" is spoken when something we interpret as good happens. Money arrives in the mail unexpectedly: "God is good!" The boss let me leave work early today: "God is good!" I found a great sale on shoes: "God is good!" My name was drawn for a door prize: "God is good!"

The phrase is used almost as a good luck charm.

God is good when blessings come our way, but also when times are hard. When he answers yes to our prayers, he is good. When he says no, he is good. When he says wait, he is good. We sometimes act like spoiled children because we don't like to hear "no" or "wait."

> God is good when blessings come our way, but also when times are hard.

So we think, *Daddy's not being nice to me!*

Even the pain God allows is filled with his goodness. When we talk about God's goodness in response to our so-called good situations, we're showing our lack of understanding. Our biggest challenge is to realize that God is good—period. Can you say, even when seemingly bad things happen, that God is good?

Our trouble is that we think God is like us and he will eventually turn on us. He will get angry. He will think bad thoughts about us. He'll get tired of us. God is good all the time. His intentions toward his children are always kind and loving.

> Even though the fig trees have no blossoms, and there are no grapes on the vine; even though the olive crop fails, and the fields lie empty and barren; even though the

> flocks die in the fields, and the cattle barns are empty, yet I will rejoice in the Lord!
> —Habakkuk 3:17 NLT

> Taste and see that the Lord is good.
> —Psalm 34:8 NLT

Tasting something is a way of finding out what it is really like. To taste God, to find out what he is really like, we need to read his Word, trust him, and obey him. Try it! As we trust him each day we will taste, that is, experience, how good God is.

He wants you to be happy. God wants you to live an abundant life. When you are surrendered to his will, God loves to please you. He is a Father filled with good thoughts toward his children and loves giving gifts to bless their lives.

> Whatever is good and perfect comes to us from God above, who created all heaven's lights.
> —James 1:17 NLT

Every gift we have comes from God the Father who loves pleasing his precious children. J.I. Packer lists some of them: "Every meal, every pleasure, every possession, every bit of sun, every night's sleep, every moment of health and safety, everything else that sustains and enriches life, is a divine gift."[2]

Instead of being skeptical and viewing God like a human being, thank God for the gifts he gives you. He is genuinely kindhearted and generous and good.

> The LORD is good to everyone. He showers compassion on all his creation.
>
> —Psalm 145:9 NLT

I Praise You Because You Are Good!

For further reading about God's goodness, read Psalm 107.

Questions for Reflection

What does a good person look like?

Psalm 16:2 (NLT) says, "All the good things I have are from you." What are some of the good things God has given you?

Can you think of a time when God said no or wait to your prayer and later you saw his goodness in it?

Copy a couple of Bible verses about God's goodness to remember when you're tempted to think otherwise about him.

Pray

Dear God, I praise you because you are good. The desires you give me and those you don't both show your goodness. Teach me to trust that you will bring good even out of situations that don't appear to be good. Thank you for the pain that you allow in my life as well as the pleasure. Help me to be aware of the many good gifts you give. You alone are good and I praise you for it! Amen.

Related Verses

> Your goodness is so great! You have stored up great blessings for those who honor you.
> —Psalm 31:19 NLT

> For the Lord is good. His unfailing love continues forever, and his faithfulness continues to each generation.
> —Psalm 100:5 NLT

> O taste and see that the Lord is good.
> —Psalm 34:8 KJV

Chapter 19

GOD IS GENEROUS

> Generosity is…the focal point of God's moral perfection; it is the quality which determines how all God's other excellences are to be displayed.[1]
> —J. I. Packer

Generous: liberal in giving or sharing; marked by abundance.

Synonyms: liberal, openhanded, giving.

> If God didn't hesitate to put everything on the line for us, embracing our condition and exposing himself to the worst by sending his own Son, is there anything else he wouldn't gladly and freely do for us?
> —Romans 8:32 MESSAGE

I remember sharing Christmas with some friends when our children were very young. Our hosts had a daughter, a toddler, and she had more Christmas presents than this little girl would ever be able to open in one day! When I asked how long it took her to complete her shopping, the mother told me she had shopped all year for this moment. Some people might classify these parents as generous. Some might say they were foolishly fond in their giving.

God is generous. He is openhanded in his giving to us for all our needs when we come to him. He is not stingy, nor does he make us beg when we come to him. Giving generously is the heart of our God.

> If you then, evil as you are, know how to give good and advantageous gifts to your children, how much more will your Father who is in heaven [perfect as he is] give good and advantageous things to those who keep on asking him!
> —Matthew 7:11 AMPLIFIED

God asked King Solomon, "What do you want? Ask, and I will give it to you!" (I Kings 3:5 NLT). Solomon asked for wisdom. He asked for an understanding mind so he would govern well and be able to know the difference between right and wrong. God answered his prayer—did he ever!

> God gave Solomon great wisdom and understanding, and knowledge too vast to be measured. In fact, his wisdom exceeded that of all the wise men of the East and the wise men of Egypt. He was wiser than anyone else, including Ethan the Ezrahite and Heman, Calcol, and Darda—the sons of Mahol. His fame spread throughout all the surrounding nations.
> —I Kings 4:29-31 NLT

God is not a "sugar daddy" who is ready to give anything for which we ask. He is not a vending machine waiting to dole out the goods when we send up a prayer. If God sees that something is good for you, he is ready to give it abundantly. He knows what we need, what we want and what we are able to handle.

Time after time in Scripture we see how generous God is. When God provided for the widow in I Kings, every jar she had gathered was filled to the brim. In Psalm 23, David says, "My cup overflows with blessings." (Psalm 23:5 NLT) Jesus fed thousands of people with a few small fish and some bread. "They all ate until they were full, and when the scraps were picked up, there were seven large baskets of food left over!" (Matthew 15:37 NLT).

Stinginess stems from insecurity and fear, neither of which is found in God's character. God's desire is to give and give in a big-hearted way. We are the ones who limit God's blessings by our disobedience or a lack of faith.

> For the LORD God is a sun and shield; The LORD will give grace and glory; No good thing will he withhold from those who walk uprightly.
> —Psalm 84:11 KJV

What do you need from God today? Which jars do you have that need to be filled? Who is waiting to be fed? He is ready to give generously. He has wisdom for that decision, healing for your sickness, relief for your pain, and provision for the empty bank account.

Let's not believe that God will give to us meagerly and only after endless pleading. God's heart is generous—in his wisdom he knows what and when to give.

God's heart is generous—in his wisdom he knows what and when to give.

> Now to him who, by (in consequence of) the [action of his] power that is at work within us, is able to [carry out his purpose and] do superabundantly, far over and above all that we [dare] ask or think [infinitely beyond our highest prayers, desires, thoughts, hopes, or dreams]. To him be glory in the church and in Christ Jesus throughout all generations forever and ever. Amen (so be it).
> —Ephesians 3:20-21 AMPLIFIED

I Praise You Because You Are Generous!

For further reading about God's generosity, read Matthew 20:1-16 and Genesis 1–2.

Questions for Reflection

Do you suffer from stinginess? What is at its root?

Reflect on a time when God generously responded to your need.

How does your situation look after thinking about God's generosity?

How will you respond to others in light of God's generosity to you?

Pray

God, you are a God of abundance! Your heart is liberal and open to me, your child. You give because you love me and want to bless me. I thank you that your generosity and your wisdom work together to give me what I need when I need it. I trust your heart toward me. Amen.

Related Verses

You crown the year with a bountiful harvest; even the hard pathways overflow with abundance.
—Psalm 65:11 NLT

Give as freely as you have received!
—Matthew 10:8 NLT

Remember this—a farmer who plants only a few seeds will get a small crop. But the one who plants generously will get a generous crop.
—2 Corinthians 9:6 NLT

Chapter 20

GOD IS PERFECT

When we apply perfection to God, we mean that he has unqualified fullness and completeness of whatever he has.[1]

—A.W. Tozer

Perfect: being entirely without fault or defect; flawless; satisfying all requirements; corresponding to an ideal standard; implies the soundness and the excellence of every part, element, or quality of a thing; frequently as an unattainable or theoretical state.

Synonyms: whole, entire, intact, flawless, faultless.

Can you find out the deep things of God, or can you by searching find out the limits of the Almighty [explore his depths, ascend to his heights, extend to his breadths, and comprehend his infinite perfection]?

—Job 11:7 AMPLIFIED

Practicing piano has never been a chore for me. In high school when the bus dropped me off at home, I'd walk straight into the house and to the piano. An hour a day of practice right after school was my regular pattern. Each scale had to be perfect. If I made a mistake, I played it again until it was flawless. Now when I'm working on a hymn arrangement, I play it over and over to work out the difficult passages. One little skip of the finger and the piece isn't perfect anymore! My definition of perfect is not hitting any wrong notes.

When I was a child, perfect for me meant free of mistakes. We call certain things perfect, but do we really mean it? It was a *perfect* sunset. That is the *perfect* outfit on you.

I found the *perfect* gift for him. Your timing is *perfect*! I got a *perfect* score on my test.

Perfect means being entirely without fault or defect. No human being is perfect. Nothing we touch, see, hear, do, eat, wear, or play will be entirely without fault or defect. We were born imperfect, and we live in an imperfect world.

How could we worship an imperfect God? God *is* perfect. He is flawless and he is complete. He needs nothing. All that God is, he is in himself—he is self-sufficient. If he needed anything or anybody, he would not be perfect. Perfection is usually about progressing to a certain level. God is in a class by himself because he is completely different and above our thinking.

God is in a class by himself because he is completely different and above our thinking.

Everything about God is perfect.

God's Word is perfect.

> The law of the LORD is perfect, reviving the soul.
> —Psalm 19:7 NLT

God's ways are perfect.

> As for God, his way is perfect. All the LORD's promises prove true.
> —Psalm 18:30 NLT

God's will is perfect.

> Don't copy the behavior and customs of this world, but let God transform you into a new person by changing the way you think. Then you will know what God wants you to do, and you will know how good and pleasing and perfect his will really is.
> —Romans 12:2 NLT

God's work is perfect.

> He is the Rock; his work is perfect. Everything he does is just and fair. He is a faithful God who does no wrong.
> —Deuteronomy 32:4 NLT

Jesus Christ, who lived a perfect life on earth, was the perfect sacrifice.

> For by the power of the eternal Spirit, Christ offered himself to God as a perfect sacrifice for our sins.
> —Hebrews 9:14 NLT

> Jesus said, "But you are to be perfect, even as your Father in heaven is perfect."
> —Matthew 5:48 NLT

God is perfect, but how is that possible for me?

Another meaning for perfect comes from the Greek word *teleios*, which means "fully grown" or "mature." A person is teleios when he is full-grown. Something is perfect if it realizes the purpose for which it was planned and designed.

A person is perfect if he fulfills the purpose for which he was created.

> Why were we created? We were created to be like God... and he chose them to become like his Son.
> —Romans 8:29 NLT

Read the verse in Matthew again.

> You, therefore, must be perfect [growing into complete maturity of godliness in mind and character, having reached the proper height of virtue and integrity], as your heavenly Father is perfect.
> —Matthew 5:48 AMPLIFIED

God isn't expecting us to live flawlessly. He is saying our behavior should match our spiritual maturity. We don't expect a two-year old to clean his room and cook dinner. However, if a twenty-two-year-old can't do that, something is wrong. God isn't expecting more of us than our stage of spiritual growth allows. Babies aren't born fully grown. They grow in stages, and sometimes spurts of growth. As we deliberately apply God's Word to our lives, accept his discipline, and give him control, we grow in Christ-likeness. Aahhhh—perfection!

> For it has pleased [the Father] that all the divine fullness (the sum total of the divine perfection, powers, and attributes) should dwell in him permanently.
> —Colossians 1:19 AMPLIFIED

I Praise You Because You Are Perfect!

To read more about God's perfection read Psalm 19.

Questions for Reflection

Are you a perfectionist? In what ways?
What does God's perfection mean to you?
Give a definition of what it means for you to be perfect in God's eyes.
Read Ephesians 4:11-13. It says we are equipped to do ministry, and serving is for "the perfecting of the saints." How will you apply these verses?

Pray

Mighty God, you are totally worthy of all my worship because you are the only one who needs no one. You are perfect in all your ways and in everything you do. I am humbled that even though you don't need us, you have chosen to invite us into relationship with you. I worship you for who you are. In your Name, Amen.

Related Verses

> He is the sole expression of the glory of God [the light-being, the out-raying or radiance of the divine], and he is the perfect imprint and very image of [God's] nature, upholding and maintaining and guiding and propelling the universe by his mighty word of power.
> —Hebrews 1:3 AMPLIFIED

> I don't mean to say that I have already achieved these things or that I have already reached perfection! But I

keep working toward that day when I will finally be all that Christ Jesus saved me for and wants me to be.
—Philippians 3:12 NLT

The one thing I ask of the LORD—the thing I seek most—is to live in the house of the LORD all the days of my life, delighting in the LORD's perfections and meditating in his temple.
—Psalm 27:4 NLT

Chapter 21

GOD IS TRUTHFUL

Truth…is his nature, and he has not got it in him to be anything else. That is why he cannot lie. That is why his words to us are true, and cannot be other than true.[1]
—J. I. Packer

Truthful: consistently telling the truth; honest; corresponding to reality; true.

Synonyms: accurate, believable, exact, factual, scrupulous.

A shepherd boy was responsible for watching the villagers' sheep. Out of boredom one day he shouted, "Wolf! Wolf!" and the people from the village came running to help chase the wolf away. This so amused him he tried it a second time with the same response. The third time he cried wolf, a wolf was indeed prowling around the sheep. This time, though, there was no response from the villagers. The last line of this fable gives us a sobering reality: "Nobody believes a liar…even when he is telling the truth."

Lying has become prevalent in our society. People lie for business advantage, for convenience, to protect themselves, for the fun of it, and to see if they can get away with it. As a little boy once said, "Lying is an abomination to God, but it is a present help in trouble!" Some people certainly agree, however lying is a refuge for weakness. Lying breeds distrust. It's hard to trust a person who has lied because you wonder if he or she will do it again.

God is truthful, but different than we are. I am a truthful person, but have I ever lied? Yes. Have I ever candy-coated the facts to make them more palatable? Yes.

God isn't just truthful—he *is* truth, the original truth, the source of all truth.

> God is not a man, that he should lie. He is not a human, that he should change his mind. Has he ever spoken and failed to act? Has he ever promised and not carried it through?
>
> —Numbers 23:19 NLT

If God weren't truthful, everything else about him would be open to question—his character, his acts, his Word. He will not lie and he cannot lie.

God's truth is revealed in Jesus. Jesus said, "I am the Way, the Truth and the Life" (John 14:6 KJV).

John described Jesus as "full of grace and truth" (John 1:14 KJV).

"'What is truth?' Pilate asked as Jesus stood before him" (John 18:38 NLT).

That seems to be the question of our day, too.

"This sounds good."

"Lots of people agree with this."

If God weren't truthful, everything else about him would be open to question—his character, his acts, his Word.

Is truth whatever the majority seems to agree with?

When people form the standard for truth, that standard keeps changing and consequently leaves us confused.

What used to be wrong is now all right. Under most circumstances, don't do it, but in this case go ahead. There are shifting standards and exceptions to the rule, and we let each person choose for himself.

No wonder people today, like Pilate, ask, "What is truth?"

The truth, God's truth, never changes.

> All Scripture is inspired by God and is useful to teach us what is true and to make us realize what is wrong in our lives.
> —II Timothy 3:16 NLT

Because God is truthful, his Word is true and trustworthy. It is our standard for testing everything else that claims to be true.

Satan is the father of lies! He hates the truth. He will water it down, bend it, embellish it, shade it, alter it, twist it, trifle with it, mince it, spin it, and stretch it. He whispers lies, and lies bring confusion.

Dishonesty takes a toll in our lives, too. The effects of dishonesty are staggering. J. I. Packer lists some results: "conscience atrophies, the sense of shame dries up, one's capacity for truthfulness, loyalty and honesty is eaten away, one's character disintegrates."[2] Enough said!

Because God is truthful and his words to us are absolutely true, you never have to read a verse in the Bible and ask,

"Did that really happen? Could those words apply to me?" When God speaks deep in your heart, don't doubt it.

> God says, "I publicly proclaim bold promises, I do not whisper obscurities in some dark corner so no one can understand what I mean. And I did not tell the people of Israel to ask me for something I did not plan to give. I, the Lord, speak only what is true and right."
> —Isaiah 45:19 NLT

The more you know the truth, the easier it will be to identify the lies.

If God had ever lied—even once, if he had not kept his Word (even once!)—I certainly would take a cautious stance and say, "God is pretty honest, but not completely." But God has never lied or gone against his Word.

He is completely truthful and you can trust him.

I Praise You Because You Are Truthful!

To read about God's Spirit of truth, read John 16:5-15.

Questions for Reflection

Have you had experience with a liar? What was the outcome?

Do you believe God's Word is entirely true? Why or why not?

Can you identify a lie Satan has tried to feed you? What was it?

How does knowing God has never lied affect your trust in him?

Pray

Dear God, your Spirit is the Spirit of truth. No matter what lies I've been told in the past, remind me you are always truthful. Give me wisdom and discernment as I read your Word so I can identify the Enemy's lies. I'm thankful I can always trust you. Amen

Related Verses

> Jesus told him, "I am the way, the truth, and the life. No one can come to the Father except through me."
> —John 14:6 NLT

> And you will know the truth, and the truth will set you free.
> —John 8:32 NLT

> Truth stands the test of time; lies are soon exposed.
> —Proverbs 12:19 NLT

Chapter 22

God Is Accessible

> He is there and he is here and everywhere...near to everything, next to everyone, and through Jesus Christ immediately accessible to every loving heart.[1]
> —A.W. Tozer

Accessible: easily approached or entered; easy to talk to or get along with.

Synonyms: approachable, available, reachable.

> So, friends, we can now—without hesitation—walk right up to God, into "the Holy Place." Jesus has cleared the way by the blood of his sacrifice, acting as our priest before God. The "curtain" into God's presence is his body.
> —Hebrews 10:19-21 MESSAGE

One summer our daughters were on a mission trip in England while my husband and I enjoyed a vacation in Hawaii. On Father's Day, as we were enjoying a lovely dinner, the cell phone rang. From halfway around the world our daughters were calling to wish their dad a happy Father's Day. It was comforting to know we could reach out and touch each other although we were thousands of miles apart.

Did you ever really need to contact someone and you couldn't? In our age of expanding technology we expect to be able to find people wherever they are. What happened to the days of leaving the kids at home with a babysitter and returning three hours later? Some people's business cards have several contact phone numbers crowded on them: home phone, business phone, cell phone, pager, fax machine. With all of these high-tech communication devices, you'd think a person could be located anytime and anywhere. Yet we still end up with voice mail, busy signals, and unanswered phone calls.

When you desperately need to talk to someone, it's frustrating to call three or four phone numbers and still not be able to reach him or her!

The mighty God of the universe, who needs no phone number, is instantly and constantly accessible to us. No call waiting. No recorded messages. No place where we are out of his range or reception is poor.

> Yes. What other great nation has gods that are intimate with them the way GOD, our God, is with us, always ready to listen to us?
> —Deuteronomy 4:7 MESSAGE

God is never too busy for us. He's never tired after a long day. He never needs to be left alone. God is never preoccupied with his own problems and uninterested in yours.

Not only is God available, we can approach him with ease. He welcomes our coming to him.

> So let us come boldly to the throne of our gracious God. There we will receive his mercy, and we will find grace to help us when we need it.
> —Hebrews 4:16 NLT

This is one of the privileges we have in a personal relationship with Jesus Christ. He says we can come confidently and boldly to him. In the Old Testament the process to approach God held many requirements. The curtain in the Jewish temple separated the place where God's presence dwelt from where the people were allowed.

Jesus' death on the cross changed that for us. Matthew 27:50 (NLT) records what happened when Jesus died: "At that moment, the curtain in the temple was torn in two, from top to bottom." God had opened the way for us to have personal access to him through Jesus Christ.

God had opened the way for us to have personal access to him through Jesus Christ.

> Let us go right into the presence of God, with true hearts fully trusting him. For our evil consciences have been sprinkled with Christ's blood to make us clean, and our bodies have been washed with pure water.
> —Hebrews 10:22 NLT

Jesus showed his approachability in the way he dealt with the crowds of people who followed him. He let the crowds press in around him throughout his ministry. In Luke 8:45, a woman in the crowd comes up behind Jesus and touches the fringe of his robe. She trembles with fear when Jesus asks, "Who touched me?" When she falls at his feet, Jesus doesn't scold her. He calls her "daughter."

He says, "Your faith has healed you" and he tells her to go in peace.

Jesus was touchable. He was ready and willing to respond when she needed him. Nothing is limiting our contact with God.

> As for me, I look to the LORD for his help. I wait confidently for God to save me, and my God will certainly hear me.
>
> —Micah 7:7 NLT

Is something on your mind? He's ready to listen.

I Praise You Because You Are Accessible!

Read Leviticus 16:1-25 to understand how different it was to approach God before Jesus came. Hebrews 10 offers more reading on our accessibility to God through Jesus.

Questions for Reflection

Tell about a time you needed to contact someone and couldn't. How did it make you feel?

In what spirit do you generally approach God?

What does it mean to you to know God is always available?

What is on your mind now to tell God?

Pray

Precious Lord Jesus, thank you for opening my access to God through your death on the cross. I can boldly come to you anytime and you welcome me. It's humbling to think that you, the God of the universe, turn your ear to me whenever I call. I love you. Amen.

Related Verses

> I love God because he listened to me, listened as I begged for mercy. He listened so intently as I laid out my case before him.
> —Psalm 116:1-2 MESSAGE

> My heart has heard you say, "Come and talk with me." And my heart responds, "Lord, I am coming."
> —Psalm 27:8 NLT

> I will call to you whenever trouble strikes, and you will answer me.
> —Psalm 86:7 NLT

Chapter 23

GOD IS EXTRAVAGANT

Because he is what he is, he lifts up our heads out of the prison house, changes our prison garments for royal robes, and makes us to eat bread continually before him all the days of our lives.[1]

—A.W. Tozer

Extravagant: exceeding reasonable bounds; extremely abundant.

Synonyms: excessive, lavish, extreme, unrestrained.

No good thing will the Lord withhold from those who do what is right.

—Psalm 84:11 NLT

Have you ever known someone who is extravagant? Without limits, unrestrained, excessive? To me, being extravagant conjures up ideas of fur coats, all-you-can-eat buffet lines, and money lavishly spent. I think of Donald Trump…the Donald. He's extravagant in his choice of homes, transportation, and jewelry. His whole lifestyle is extravagant. When you think about it, even his hairstyle is extravagant.

God is extravagant.

Just look at the colors in a sunset. Have you ever sat on the beach and listened to the crashing ocean waves? On a clear night, look up at the sky full of stars as far as your eyes can see. Think about a newborn baby—a perfect human being in miniature! The way a human heart works is incredible.

God is extravagant in what he has created.

The story of the prodigal son in Luke 15 is about a young man who asks his dad for his inheritance. He spends it all wastefully, and disgraces and disrespects his dad, only to find his father waiting for him with open arms, running to him, when he finally returns. This is a picture of God's extravagant forgiveness. The woman in John 12 who lavished expensive perfume on Jesus' feet knew how extravagant his forgiveness was.

God is extravagant in his forgiveness.

God allowed his only child, his Son Jesus, to die a cruel death to pay the penalty for our sins. His whole purpose was to bring about reconciliation between him and us. That is extravagant love.

> Listen to these extravagant phrases about God:
> The generosity of his gracious favor, which he lavished upon us in every kind of wisdom and understanding.
> —Ephesians 1:7-8 AMPLIFIED

> Oh, the utter extravagance of his work in us who trust him—endless energy, boundless strength.
> —Ephesians 1:19 MESSAGE

> The unending (boundless, fathomless, incalculable, and exhaustless) riches of Christ [wealth which no human being could have searched out], the unending riches of Christ.
> —Ephesians 3:8 AMPLIFIED

God Is Extravagant • 165

> Where sin increased and abounded, grace (God's unmerited favor) has surpassed it and increased the more and superabounded.
> —Romans 5:20 AMPLIFIED

> I came that they may have and enjoy life and have it in abundance (to the full, till it overflows).
> —John 10:10 AMPLIFIED

God does things in a big way: creating the heavens and earth, filling the widow's empty jars with enough oil to sell it and live on the profit, feeding more than 5,000 people from a tiny lunch, and filling the disciples' fishing nets to overflowing after they'd fished all night with no results. His promises to take care of us and supply our needs are sweeping, abundant, and luxurious—not just adequate.

God doesn't want his kids living at the poverty level—spiritually or emotionally. Worry, small thinking, fear, and guilt just don't line up with the extravagant love, forgiveness, and provision God has for us. Lay back on that big fluffy pillow of God's love and forgiveness and provision—and rest.

> God doesn't want his kids living at the poverty level—spiritually or emotionally.

Praise God for his extravagance.

We need his extravagant love, forgiveness, and reconciliation.

Much more than homes, cars and jewelry!

> Now to him who is able to do immeasurably more than all we ask or imagine, according to his power that is at work within us, to him be glory in the church and in Christ Jesus throughout all generations, for ever and ever! Amen.
>
> —Ephesians 3:20-21 NLT

I Praise You Because You Are Extravagant!

To read how God answered Elijah's prayer in an extravagant way, read I Kings 18.

Questions for Reflection

Do you know someone who is extravagant in his or her lifestyle, giving, or in some other way?

Record a way you've observed God's extravagance.

What are you worrying about that God has already extravagantly provided for you?

In light of God's extravagance, how will you live?

Pray

God, as I look around, evidence of your extravagance is everywhere. It's not only in what you have created, but also in the ways you deal with me. You love me and forgive me without limit. You promise to take care of me. Help me to live the abundant life you've promised. For your glory, Amen.

Related Verses

Then the LORD brought Abram outside beneath the night sky and told him, "Look up into the heavens and count the stars if you can. Your descendants will be like that—too many to count!"

—Genesis 15:5 NLT

The people of Israel had walked through the middle of the sea on dry land, as the water stood up like a wall on both sides.

—Exodus 14:29 NLT

You can ask for anything in my name, and I will do it, because the work of the Son brings glory to the Father.

—John 14:13 NLT

Chapter 24

GOD IS LOYAL

The secret to a life of unending joy and peace involves finding something or someone who will "come through" for you 100 percent of the time in any and every situation forever.[1]

—Chip Ingram

Loyal: faithful to a private person to whom fidelity is held to be due; showing loyalty, faithful to a cause, ideal or custom; implies a firm resistance to any temptation to desert or betray.

Synonyms: allegiant, attached, constant, dependable, devoted, dutiful, steadfast, steady, true, true-blue, trustworthy, unfailing, unswerving, unwavering.

"For the mountains may depart and the hills disappear, but even then I will remain loyal to you. My covenant of blessing will never be broken," says the LORD who has mercy on you.

—Isaiah 54:10 NLT

What kind of word picture comes to your mind when you think of the word *loyal*? I think of a friend who will stick with you in the happy and sad times. Or an employee who will work long past the normal workday hours to finish the job if that's what it takes. Or a dog that will not leave its master's side in stormy weather or darkness.

Loyal friends are irreplaceable. You can count on them to be there for you in tough times. You know they will keep your secrets. They know you well and still love you. Loyalty in an employee is a sterling characteristic. One who is dependable takes pressure off his or her employer.

> Putting confidence in an unreliable person is like chewing with a toothache or walking on a broken foot.
> —Proverbs 25:19 NLT

Proverbs 19:22 gives us an interesting insight: "Loyalty makes a person attractive. And it is better to be poor than dishonest" (NLT). Proverbs is a book of practical ethics. It is poetry that uses parallelism in thought in different ways. In this verse, the second line of the couplet amplifies the thought of the first. Solomon is linking loyalty with honesty. A person who is disloyal cannot be depended on to be trustworthy in his or her allegiance. Loyalty is an unselfish characteristic because it means working through problems instead of walking out.

Loyalty is the mark of genuine friendship and God is the ultimate loyal friend. He won't leave us when there is a communication problem. He won't desert us if we don't pray enough. He won't give up on us even if we give up on him. He is not a fair-weather friend!

>
> Loyalty is the mark of genuine friendship and God is the ultimate loyal friend.
>

> "I will be your God throughout your lifetime—until your hair is white with age. I made you, and I will care for you. I will carry you along and save you."
> —Isaiah 46:4 NLT

God has promised over and over in his Word always to be there for us. That kind of dependability brings us comfort and security. Those who have dealt with rejection or abandonment can find it hard to trust these kinds of promises. His promises can be depended on because they are backed by all the honor of God's name.

> Your promises are backed by all the honor of your name.
> —Psalm 138:2 NLT

No matter what path your life may take, Jesus' steady love will always be yours. When your hopes are shattered, when someone you love is no longer with you, when you have failed the Lord, He will still be there for you.

He won't reject you. He won't walk out on you. He won't change his mind.

> "Yet Jerusalem says, 'The Lord has deserted us; the Lord has forgotten us.' Never! Can a mother forget her nursing child? Can she feel no love for a child she has borne? But even if that were possible, I would not forget you!
> —Isaiah 49:15-16 NLT

God's loyalty and devotion to us is further proof of his unending love—in stormy weather or darkness.

I Praise You Because You Are Loyal!

Read Jeremiah 31 for more of God's words of loyalty to you.

Questions for Reflection

What is your definition of a loyal friend?
Who in your life has been dependable and constant?
Choose a verse that speaks of God's loyalty to you and record it here.
In a world of so much change, why is God's loyalty important to you?

Pray

Precious Lord, thank you for the security of your loyal love and care. Your Word tells me you will never leave me no matter what happens in my life. You are the constant in my life. I am thankful to be your child. I praise you for always being there for me. I love you. Amen.

Related Verses

> "Don't be afraid, I've redeemed you, I've called your name. You're mine. When you're in over your head, I'll be there with you."
> —Isaiah 43:1-2 MESSAGE

> For God has said, "I will never fail you. I will never forsake you."
> —Hebrews 13:5 NLT

After that I saw heaven opened, and behold, a white horse [appeared]! The one who was riding it is called Faithful (Trustworthy, Loyal, Incorruptible, Steady) and True, and he passes judgment and wages war in righteousness (holiness, justice, and uprightness).

—Revelation 19:11 AMPLIFIED

Chapter 25

GOD IS GRACIOUS

Mercy is not receiving something that we deserve, and grace is receiving something that we don't deserve.[1]
—Steve McVey

Gracious: characterized by kindness and warm courtesy; of a merciful or compassionate nature; enjoying favor or grace; acceptable or pleasing.

Synonyms: approachable, benevolent, bighearted, considerate, giving, kind.

The Word became flesh and made his dwelling among us. We have seen his glory, the glory of the one and only, who came from the Father, full of grace and truth.
—John 1:14 NIV

At our first pastorate we had a family in the church who raised cattle. When we arrived in town they told us they would give us some beef when they next butchered. But there was a condition. We had to help them eat the old beef first. They had a cow that had gotten caught in a barbed wire fence and died. The animal hadn't been properly bled and butchered so all the meat was made into hamburger—very bad-tasting hamburger. I tried every way I could think of to disguise the terrible taste: adding sauce, spices—even Hamburger Helper couldn't help it!

We didn't "deserve" the good meat until we "earned" it by helping to eat the bad hamburger.

Some people think God operates on this principle: you'll deserve it as soon as you pay your dues. When you have done enough good things, I might let you into heaven. Some others think God works by this adage: one good turn deserves another. You've followed most of the Ten Commandments and gone to church when you could so I'll let you into heaven. Earning our way is an American value so it's quite easy to buy into those statements. However, these are not what the Bible teaches.

God is gracious, that is, he is full of kindness and love. That means two important things for us. First, because of his kindness and goodness he freely forgives our sins. It isn't because of anything we've done or can do. We don't deserve to have our sins forgiven. God does this because he is gracious.

> For all have sinned; all fall short of God's glorious standard. Yet now God in his gracious kindness declares us not guilty.
> —Romans 3:23 NLT

Second, God freely gives us his power to live for him because he knows we are incapable of doing it on our own. After we've accepted Christ, we want to live for him. Desire is not the problem. It's the ability to do so. In the way we act sometimes we seem to be saying, "Thanks for saving me, God, but I can take it from here."

We try so hard to follow God's rules. We try and fail, then try and fail some more. Then we feel discouraged and want to give up. Or we think God will love us more if we pray or read our Bibles more. God, full of grace, wants to give us his power to live for him. It's about accepting his power and leaning on him daily. He wants us to trust him and simply rest in him, instead of trying in our own strength.

He wants us to trust him and simply rest in him, instead of trying in our own strength.

> But he gives us more and more grace (power of the Holy Spirit, to meet this evil tendency and all others fully).
> —James 4:6 AMPLIFIED

The difference is where we place our focus. When we start counting how many days we missed reading our Bibles, it robs us of victory. God wants us to focus our thoughts on him to perpetuate our love and intimacy with him. If he loved you enough to freely forgive your sins—for no other reason than because he chose to do so—he is not standing with a stick ready to beat you for sinning. He wants to give freely to you again. Now he wants to give you the power you need each day. Concentrate on Jesus, and on how much he loves you and how kind he is to freely give you wonderful gifts.

When our children were young, they helped with chores around the house and they were given an allowance. The two were not connected, however. They weren't paid an allowance for doing chores. They helped with chores because they were part of the family. They were given an allowance because they were our children. We wanted their motivation to be love and thanks instead of duty. God wants us to be motivated by love for him and thanks for what he has done for us. Our lifestyle will flow from our relationship with him.

I can stand free and not condemned because God is gracious in forgiving me.

I can rest instead of trying harder because God is gracious in empowering me.

I can live in confidence and boldness because God is incredibly kind, unbelievably good, and immensely loving.

> And therefore the Lord [earnestly] waits [expecting, looking, and longing] to be gracious to you; and therefore he lifts himself up, that he may have mercy on you and show loving-kindness to you. For the Lord is a God of justice. Blessed (happy, fortunate, to be envied) are all those who [earnestly] wait for him, who expect and look and long for him [for his victory, his favor, his love, his peace, his joy, and his matchless, unbroken companionship]!
>
> —Isaiah 30:18 AMPLIFIED

I Praise You Because You Are Gracious!

To understand more about God's graciousness, read Romans 5 and 6.

Questions for Reflection

Why do people try to earn their ways to heaven?

What is the only way to be saved (Ephesians 2:8-9)?

What is your motivation in doing good things for God?

How does your life reflect your love for Christ?

Pray

Precious Lord, what can I say about your overflowing favor? You have freely pardoned my sins. I did nothing to earn that. Thank you for graciously forgiving me. Once again you want to freely give me your grace, now to live victoriously for you each day. Help me to understand my relationship with you is one of love and not obligation. I want to fall in love with you more and more. Amen.

Related Verses

> The Lord is merciful and gracious, slow to anger and plenteous in mercy and loving-kindness.
> —Psalm 103:8 AMPLIFIED

> Those who think they can do it on their own end up obsessed with measuring their own moral muscle but never get around to exercising it in real life. Those who trust God's action in them find that God's Spirit is in them—living and breathing God!
> —Romans 8:5-6 MESSAGE

> Each time he said, "My gracious favor is all you need. My power works best in your weakness." So now I am glad to boast about my weaknesses, so that the power of Christ may work through me.
> —2 Corinthians 12:9 NLT

Chapter 26

GOD IS CREATIVE

"In the beginning God created"—but before the beginning, there wasn't any "beginning;" there wasn't any "before!"[1]

—A.W. Tozer

Creative: having the power or quality to bring into existence; having the quality of something created rather than imitated.

Synonyms: inspired, innovative, artistic, original, inventive.

The LORD merely spoke, and the heavens were created. He breathed the word, and all the stars were born.

—Psalm 33:6 NLT

Creating is an exhilarating process for me. I love it so much that I'm frustrated if I'm not creating something. I'm not content just to follow a recipe or sew from a pattern. I want to customize and invent. It's fun to look at a book of house plans, but I would rather draw my own. I want to arrange my own piano solos instead of playing an arrangement from a book.

We can become quite proud of our creative ideas, solutions, and inventions, but at their best they are still only human ideas. My "creative" ideas, although they seem original to me, no doubt came from something else I tasted, saw, or heard.

God is creative. When he brings something into being, he isn't copying anything else—it's all original! We're talking about stars, planets, and even galaxies! While we keep ourselves busy exploring one star—Earth—the Creator of the stars "counts them to see that none are lost" "calling each by its name" Isaiah 40:26 (NLT).

> He is the one who made heaven and earth, the sea, and everything in them. He is the one who keeps every promise forever.
> —Psalm 146:6 NLT

Then there's God's amazing creation: man. He created us because he wanted a relationship with us. God's deepest desire is to have a personal relationship with each of us.

> And the LORD God formed a man's body from the dust of the ground and breathed into it the breath of life. And the man became a living person.
> —Genesis 2:7 NLT

Whatever God creates is magnificent. The earth rotates exactly on schedule. The human body is incredibly intricate. For example, think about just one part of your body, such as your ear. Inside your inner ear are some 20,000 hair cells with filaments in varying lengths, much like harp strings. These are the sensory hearing cells that are connected to the auditory nerve. Who else but God could create our incredible bodies?

We labor, we strain, and we tax our brains to create something. God merely spoke and the heavens were created. He just breathed the word and it happened! He formed a man's body out of dust. The Hebrew word for create, *bara*, means creation out of nothing.

Praise God that he is creative! The creation story in Genesis is amazing and it shows us who God is. It shows us his tremendous power. He is sovereign; he originates and regulates all things. If God can create a universe out of nothing, he can provide a solution to your hopeless situation. God has the most amazing creative solutions to your problems. Talk about thinking outside the box!

If God can create a universe out of nothing, he can provide a solution to your hopeless situation.

To create also means to produce through artistic or imaginative effort. God's creations are certainly artistic and imaginative. Just look at the rhinoceros or the giraffe, and over 350,000 species of beetles—how many ways can you put wings and legs on a body?

If God the Creator lives in me, I can be creative. He can breathe his breath into me to write songs, paint landscapes, design clothes, and communicate creatively. Ask God to sanctify your imagination and use it to bring him glory. Let him use you to spark ideas in whatever you're doing for him.

He's creator of all you can see or imagine.
—Isaiah 40:28 MESSAGE

Yet you have forgotten the LORD, your creator, the one who put the stars in the sky and established the earth. Will you remain in constant dread of human oppression? Will you continue to fear the anger of your enemies from morning till night? Soon all you captives will be released! Imprisonment, starvation, and death will not be your fate! For I am the LORD your God, who stirs up the sea, causing its waves to roar. My name is the LORD Almighty.
—Isaiah 51:13-15 NLT

I Praise You Because You Are Creative!

For further study, read Genesis 1 and 2.

Questions for Reflection

Do you consider yourself a creative person? Why or why not?

What does God's creativity tell you about him?

Record a time when God's creativity answered a prayer for you.

What do you need God to create in or for you?

Pray

Mighty God, by your power the heavens were created. You created man from dust. Everything you do is superb and I praise your mighty power. I know you can create solutions for my problems too. In Jesus' name, Amen.

Related Verses

You placed the world on its foundation so it would never be moved.

—Psalm 104:5 NLT

It is the LORD who created the stars, the Pleiades and Orion. It is he who turns darkness into morning and day into night. It is he who draws up water from the oceans and pours it down as rain on the land. The LORD is his name!

—Amos 5:8 NLT

From the time the world was created, people have seen the earth and sky and all that God made.

—Romans 1:20 NLT

Chapter 27

God Is Majestic

> The Christian's instincts of trust and worship are stimulated very powerfully by knowledge of the greatness of God.[1]
>
> —J. I. Packer

Majestic: having or showing lofty dignity or nobility; stately.

Synonyms: august, awesome, exalted, grand, magnificent, marvelous.

> In your majesty, ride out to victory, defending truth, humility, and justice. Go forth to perform awe-inspiring deeds!
>
> —Psalm 45:4 NLT

Without a king or queen in the U.S., it's a little bit difficult for us to get a grasp on what royalty is like. You can compete to become the Persimmon Festival Queen, the Little Miss Mermaid Queen, the Lamb and Wool Queen, or the Watermelon Queen. The contests are endless if you want to become a royal. Our idea of royalty has been devalued because anyone can become a king or queen of some sort—if he or she enters a contest, writes an essay, or gets enough votes. I was a princess once—at my high school's homecoming in 1967.

The importance of being a ruling monarch depends on over what you're ruling. If you're reigning over the county fair, your domain may be a hog-calling contest. For some people, their knowledge of royalty comes mostly from watching *Cinderella* or *Snow White*.

A king is addressed as "Your Majesty." To see him walk by would be incredible. To be in the same room with him would be an awesome experience. Although the idea of royalty is foreign to us, God's majestic nature need not be.

The word *majesty* means greatness. The Bible uses it to express the greatness of God. It means God is big!

In our society, we are obsessed with big. The average American home today is almost three times larger than in the fifties. In 1985, only 2 percent of the vehicles sold in the U.S. were SUVs. Now it's 25 percent.[2] We choose to supersize because we think bigger is better. If only we would apply that to our thinking about God. If we actually believe God is big enough to take care of all our problems, why do we worry?

This is precisely where our trouble begins. We don't think big enough thoughts about God. We generally talk about our problems and think small thoughts about God.

We hope God can do something.

We have our back-up plan ready if God doesn't come through for us.

We think God probably isn't interested in *this* situation.

People who know their God are daring in their faith. They know he is big enough to handle anything. They know he is 100 percent faithful to his promises. This is the God to whom we pray. So don't tell God how big your problems are. Instead, tell your problems how big God is.

When we say, "How majestic is your name in all the earth," we are saying how great God's name is in all the earth. Praising God for his majesty and his greatness is supremely important! Speak about his majesty—praise him for it! When we speak of how great God is, fears and doubts will diminish. Our faith will become bolder. To speak of God's greatness inspires a sense of worship and produces awe in his presence, and it humbles us. Songwriters have tried to pen words to describe just how big, great, marvelous, and wonderful God is. In reality we have no words fit to describe so majestic a King.

To speak of God's greatness inspires a sense of worship and produces awe in his presence, and it humbles us.

The Hebrew word *addir* means "mighty, majestic." The first time this word occurs in the Bible is in Exodus 15. It describes God's superior and majestic holiness demonstrated when he delivered the children of Israel from Egyptian bondage.

> Who among the gods is like you, O LORD? Who is like you—majestic in holiness, awesome in glory, working wonders?
> —Exodus 15:11 NIV

Our King carries all the superior powers you would expect of a king. God's power doesn't end at the boundary line of a country. He is King of Kings and Lord of Lords, over all principalities and powers!

Praise him for his majesty! What a privilege it is to worship our God of splendor and dignity and superior power.

> Everything he does reveals his glory and majesty. His righteousness never fails.
> —Psalm 111:3 NLT

I Praise You Because You Are Majestic!

For further reading on God's majesty, read Isaiah 40.

Questions for Reflection

What was your closest encounter with royalty?
What causes you to think small thoughts about God?
Take some time and think about how big God is. Record your thoughts.
How do your problems look in light of God's majesty?

Pray

Glorious God, I confess I have often made my problems bigger by concentrating on them more than on you. You have all the power needed for any situation. Help me to think big thoughts about you. I praise your majesty! Amen.

Related Verses

> O Lord our Lord, how majestic is your name in all the earth.
> —Psalm 8:1 NIV

> You are glorious and more majestic than the everlasting mountains.
> —Psalm 76:4 NLT

> Your throne is founded on two strong pillars—righteousness and justice. Unfailing love and truth walk before you as attendants.
> —Psalm 89:14 NLT

Chapter 28

GOD IS INFINITE

> God, being infinite, must possess attributes about which we can know nothing.[1]
>
> —A.W. Tozer

Infinite: having no boundaries or limits; immeasurably great or large; boundless.

Synonyms: absolute, immeasurable, incalculable, inestimable, inexhaustible, limitless, measureless, never-ending.

> Take a long, hard look. See how great he is—infinite, greater than anything you could ever imagine or figure out!
>
> —Job 36:26 MESSAGE

I felt incredibly silly retelling the story again and again. I tripped over a metal sign and fell in the parking lot while leaving the church one wintry night. I landed on my elbow and now my arm was in a sling. With a strained tendon, I couldn't straighten my arm completely or rotate my forearm. If I had fallen on the ice it would've made a good story, but I tripped over a metal sign. This little accident severely limited me. I couldn't continue with my daily routine. Holding a writing utensil was impossible for a few days. I couldn't play the piano for several weeks.

We are limited in many ways. We experience physical limitations due to accidents, illness, or aging. Our physical stamina becomes more limited as our years increase. We may be limited in our knowledge, perhaps due to the amount of education we've had. We may be limited in our capabilities as well.

God is not limited. He is infinite. He has no restrictions.

> Who else has held the oceans in his hand? Who has measured off the heavens with his fingers? Who else knows the weight of the earth or has weighed out the mountains and the hills?
> —Isaiah 40:12 NLT

No one but God holds these credentials. He is unique.

> To whom will you compare me? Who is my equal?
> —Isaiah 46:5 NLT

We have too small a view of God. I don't know where or how we began taking a smaller view of God, but it is exactly what Satan wants. When we minimize who God is or what he can do, we play right into Satan's hand. God is so much greater than we realize! Our minds cannot grasp this concept entirely. We must believe God is who he says he is. We are people who like to figure things out. However, some of God's aspects are beyond our comprehension.

The Scripture says, "the Spirit who lives in you is greater than the spirit who lives in the world" (I John 4:4 NIV). This is true. However, it's easy to get into a comparison mindset.

Greater than/less than.

As much as/more than.

Those are comparison words. God is the one and only God. He cannot be compared with anyone. He is not the opposite of Satan. He's not at the top of a list of rulers. He stands alone as the Supreme Ruler of all. When words like *greater than* are used in Scripture, it helps us understand what God and his power are like. We're still trapped in our framework of time and space, and God is beyond all this.

> LORD, there is no one like you! For you are great, and your name is full of power. Who would not fear you, O King of nations? That title belongs to you alone! Among all the wise people of the earth and in all the kingdoms of the world, there is no one like you.
> —Jeremiah 10:6-7 NLT

Knowing that God is unlimited brings us great peace. He is endless in his power, his wisdom, his strength, his mercy, his love, and his resources. Our fears can be put to rest knowing our big God is in charge and lovingly watching over us. There is no end to God—infinity cannot be measured. Even though we cannot comprehend God completely, it's enough to know he loves each of us personally. He is ready to provide whatever we need as we humbly come to him.

> Our fears can be put to rest knowing our big God is in charge and lovingly watching over us.

Walk outside and look at the sky. We're only seeing a few miles of our vast universe. Even if we could fly through outer space to another planet, we are still limited in space. Our measurements, from inches to light years, have no meaning to God. He is measureless. He is incomparable. No wonder we worship him.

I Praise You Because You Are Infinite!

Read more about God's unlimited capabilities in Psalm 145.

Questions for Reflection

What would it mean to you to have no limitations?
Why is God's infinite understanding of you important?
Why is God's infinite power essential?
What does it tell you about God knowing that he is both infinite and intimate?

Pray

O God, how I praise you, the one and only! As your creation, I am limited in many ways. You are infinite, and that is more than my mind can understand. But Father, because I trust you, it's enough just to know you love me. With a grateful heart, Amen.

Related Verses

I pray that from his glorious, unlimited resources he will give you mighty inner strength through his Holy Spirit.

—Ephesians 3:16 NLT

Our Lord is great, with limitless strength; we'll never comprehend what he knows and does.

—Psalm 147:5 MESSAGE

Even perfection has its limits, but your commands have no limit.

—Psalm 119:96 NLT

Chapter 29

God Is Patient

God is never in a hurry; if we wait, we shall see that God is pointing out that we have not been interested in himself but only in his blessings.[1]

—Oswald Chambers

Patient: marked by or exhibiting calm endurance of pain, difficulty, provocation, or annoyance; tolerant; understanding; manifesting forbearance under provocation or strain; not hasty or impetuous; steadfast despite opposition, difficulty or adversity; able or willing to bear.

Synonyms: longsuffering, endurance, forbearance, characterized by this divine virtue or spiritual fruit.

Don't you realize how kind, tolerant, and patient God is with you? Or don't you care? Can't you see how kind he has been in giving you time to turn from your sin?

—Romans 2:4 NLT

Do you like to wait? Most of us hate waiting. It is said that we spend one year of our lives waiting—at stoplights, in office reception areas, in line at the grocery checkout, and on the phone.

Smart businesses respect people's time. They realize people don't like to wait. Call waiting has been added to our phone options, and the express lane at the grocery store lets you scan your own groceries. It takes a long time to get a real person on the phone sometimes, but at least you don't feel like you're waiting. You are doing *something*—pressing options!

Praise God because he is patient! He is much more patient with us than we are with ourselves. His will is for us to become more like him. That formation is one long process! Even though we are slow at learning the lessons he is teaching us, even though our stubbornness dies hard, and even though we want to do what's right but don't get it right—he waits. When we don't show a Christ-like spirit in a certain situation, God has a way of arranging circumstances so we'll have another opportunity to learn that lesson.

Sometimes we feel like Paul in Romans 7.

> No matter which way I turn, I can't make myself do right. I want to, but I can't. When I want to do good, I don't. And when I try not to do wrong, I do it anyway…It seems to be a fact of life that when I want to do what is right, I inevitably do what is wrong. I love God's law with all my heart.
>
> —Romans 7:19, 21 NLT

When we feel like that, we need to remember God is extremely patient with us while we are in process. Suppose your baby was making an attempt to take his first steps. He immediately falls down. Now what? Do you say, "Well, you'll never learn to walk?" God keeps working with us, too. He knows the battle we have with our natural desires, our flesh. While God does not approve of our sin, he waits for us to make a choice and to ask him for help. He wants us to depend on his Spirit for strength to make the right choice.

God is patiently waiting for those who have not turned to him yet.

> The Lord isn't really being slow about his promise to return, as some people think. No, he is being patient for your sake. He does not want anyone to perish, so he is giving more time for everyone to repent.
> —1 Peter 3:9 NLT

He loves us so much that he doesn't want anyone to spend eternity without him. He is patiently allowing a little more time for people to turn to him.

Sadly, most of the time we do not show the same kind of patience. We give up on people. We may give someone a second chance. Maybe even one more. We may wait thirty minutes past the appointed time to meet. We may overlook that mistake one more time—but that's it!

Because patience is a Christ-like trait, God allows problems in our lives to help us become more patient. Sometimes he does this through people, sometimes through unwanted delays or other hardships. Look for God's bigger plan. His

Because patience is a Christ-like trait, God allows problems in our lives to help us become more patient.

goal is to make us "strong in character and ready for anything" (James 1:4 NLT).

A deeper love for God should develop as we see his patience with us. We should be humbled by his patient care. No matter where we are in our walks with God, he is extraordinarily patient with us.

I Praise You Because You Are Patient!

Read about God's patience with the children of Israel in Psalm 78.

Questions for Reflection

What do you think is at the root of impatience?

With whom or in what situation do you need patience?

Is there a lesson God is patiently trying to teach you?

What is your response to God's patience with you?

Pray

God, if I don't learn the lesson the first time, you don't become exasperated. You aren't standing with arms crossed, tapping your foot and raising your voice. You lovingly and gently continue the process of teaching and growing me. Thank you for your unending patience. In your name, Amen.

Related Verses

> Wherefore seeing we also are compassed about with so great a cloud of witnesses, let us lay aside every weight, and the sin which doth so easily beset us, and let us run with patience the race that is set before us.
> —Hebrews 12:1 KJV

> [We pray] that you may be invigorated and strengthened with all power according to the might of his glory, [to exercise] every kind of endurance and patience with joy.
> —Colossians 1:11 AMPLIFIED

> I pray that the Lord will guide you to be as loving as God and as patient as Christ.
> —2 Thessalonians 3:5 CEV

Chapter 30

GOD IS GENTLE

How can we turn down an invitation to trade in a heavy burden for a light load? To be taught by the Master Teacher who is humble and gentle is a high privilege.[1]
—Cynthia Heald

Gentle: considerate or kindly in disposition; amiable and tender; not harsh or severe.

Synonyms: compassionate, kind, meek, merciful, peaceful, sweet-tempered, tender, warmhearted.

You protect me with salvation-armor; you hold me up with a firm hand, caress me with your gentle ways.
—Psalm 18:35 MESSAGE

Years ago my husband and I ate breakfast at a favorite spot. Some friends recommended this little place because we'd never have found it otherwise. Nancy's Food Cellar wasn't at all what it appeared to be from the outside. It was a tiny building in a parking lot behind a mall with a homemade sign on top. A person could easily pass it without realizing it. Nancy's accommodated only about six tables and they were squeezed into the small space. It was a hole in the wall. But the omelets were magnificent. Fluffy and filled with three kinds of cheese and other goodies, they were big enough for two people to eat until they were full. Nancy's was plain on the outside but a rich experience inside. Did you ever visit a place that was a rich experience once you got inside?

The word *gentle* is a rich word once you get inside. It is much different than it appears on the surface. We think we know its meaning but it's much richer than we think. A gentle touch, gentle words. It sounds like it should belong to little children or old ladies, weak and mild.

God is gentle. The biblical definition of gentleness is anything but weak. The only time in Scripture Jesus ever spoke words to describe himself he said, "I am humble and gentle" (Matthew 11:29 NLT). Gentleness is listed as meekness in some translations. It is paired with humility in this passage and it is a twin to humility. Gentleness is about restraint instead of bluntness. It's about keeping your emotions under control instead of giving someone a piece of your mind. It's about getting angry for the right reasons at the right time. It's about being open to God and his will for you.

Jesus said he was gentle and he showed it. When a woman was caught in adultery, Jesus showed strength and restraint: "Where are your accusers? Go and sin no more" (John 8:10-11 NLT). When the moneychangers were doing big business outside the temple, Jesus became angry at the injustice. "The Scriptures declare, 'My temple will be called a place of prayer for all nations,' but you have turned it into a den of thieves" (Mark 11:17 NLT). When Jesus agonized in Gethsemane he accepted God's plan. "Please take this cup of suffering away from me. Yet I want your will, not mine" (Mark 14:36 NLT).

Gentleness has nothing to do with weakness. It is a strength displayed when a person is confident in who he is. It is a proper submission in relating to other people.

It is a characteristic of tremendous strength. Which takes more strength—to react to an insult or restrain yourself? To become annoyed over an interruption in your schedule or readjust your plans? To take revenge on the driver who cut in front of you or calmly slow down and let him pass? The Bible further defines gentleness as acting with restraint, reasonableness, a readiness to forgive, and a sweetness of disposition. The weak person will react, get revenge, rant, and demand his rights.

Because humility is at the root of gentleness, the gentle person will not be overly sensitive about himself, or defensive. A gentle person shows respect and consideration for others. A gentle person won't be selfish or proud because of what Christ has done in his heart. Gentleness will always show in his relationships with others.

> Be humble and gentle. Be patient with each other, making allowance for each other's faults because of your love.
> —Ephesians 4:2 NLT

True gentleness can't be counterfeited. It is produced by the Holy Spirit and generated from the inside. It is a spirit that accepts God's ways in our lives. Rather than complaining about circumstances, a gentle spirit will humbly accept what God allows. It is content to leave everything that happens in the hands of God.

When we lived in North Dakota, gigantic sunflower fields could be seen along the highways in the summertime. The first time we drove past a field of the bright yellow faces, I was in awe at the breathtaking sight. As the season wore on, the sunflower blossoms became heavy with seeds. As they become heavy they are no longer able to hold up their heads. When they are full of fruit, their heads are bowed and their colorful blossoms no longer show. The big talkers, the sarcastic and quick to condemn are the weak ones—colorful and empty-headed. The gentle are humble, patient, and understanding. They won't make a lot of noise, but their lives are full of fruit for the Master.

The world we live in is brusque and blunt. Most people would rather assert their opinions than arrest their tongues or explode with a reaction instead of exercising restraint. Praise God for his strong gentleness. We're never stronger than when we're gentle.

>
> Rather than complaining about circumstances, a gentle spirit will humbly accept what God allows.
>

Let your gentleness be evident to all.
—Philippians 4:5 NIV

I Praise You Because You Are Gentle!

Read Isaiah 42 for a picture of the gentleness of Jesus.

Questions for Reflection

Describe what being gentle means to you.
What do gentleness and humility have in common?
Do you think there is a lack of gentleness in our world today? Why or why not?
In what ways do you need to become more gentle?

Pray

Dear Lord, it's so easy to explode when I get angry. I want to be a gentle person as you have shown and as your Word tells me. You modeled gentleness perfectly. I submit myself completely to you and ask you to change my heart. Give me the strength to be gentle. In your name, Amen.

Related Verses

Look at my servant…he will be gentle—he will not shout or raise his voice in public. He will not crush those who are weak or quench the smallest hope.
—Isaiah 42:1-3 NLT

Since God chose you to be the holy people whom he loves, you must clothe yourselves with tenderhearted mercy, kindness, humility, gentleness, and patience.
—Colossians 3:12 NLT

A gentle answer turns away wrath, but harsh words stir up anger.
—Proverbs 15:1 NLT

Chapter 31

GOD IS IMPARTIAL

> He has no favorites within his household. All he has ever done for any of his children he will do for all of his children.[1]
>
> —A.W. Tozer

Impartial: not partial or biased; unprejudiced.

Synonyms: equal, fair, even-handed, non-discriminating, unprejudiced, unslanted.

> For God shows no partiality [undue favor or unfairness; with him one man is not different from another].
>
> —Romans 2:11 AMPLIFIED

Our home was never without pets when I was growing up. Summer afternoons with my collie were spent running, jumping, and playing games. Lancer was big and strong, but he loved to chase cars. One day it happened—he was hit by a car and had to be euthanized. My brother, sister, and I sobbed loudly for a solid hour.

Some time later we also lost our family cat. Feeling the need to be impartial, I gathered my siblings saying, "Don't you think we should cry as hard for Meringue as we did for Lancer?"

If we sense the need to be impartial, even as children, aren't you glad God is impartial? He has no favorites. He sees all of us as equals. He isn't biased or prejudiced in any way. He loves us all the same: "For God so loved the world" (John 3:16 NIV). He doesn't love only those who love him back. He doesn't love only those who give an offering. We all come to him on an equal basis. The person who serves faithfully at the soup kitchen isn't loved any more by God than the person coming to eat there. God doesn't take sides. He doesn't show special favor to one person over another or one group over another. In God we see what true untainted love is.

Try an experiment. The next time you go to the mall, go in shabby clothes and don't comb your hair. See how many clerks go out of their way to wait on you. Then try again and go in your best clothes—decked out! Partiality is nothing new. If you were raised in a home where favoritism was shown, you know how hurtful it can be. One child gets preferential treatment. One child gets away with misbehaving. One child is allowed more privileges. Favoritism took place in the Bible, and the Bible doesn't cover up the mess it caused. It is divisive in family relationships.

> Isaac loved Esau in particular because of the wild game he brought home, but Rebekah favored Jacob.
> —Genesis 25:28 NLT

> So Jacob slept with Rachel, too, and he loved her more than Leah.
> —Genesis 29:30 NLT

> Now Jacob loved Joseph more than any of his other children because Joseph had been born to him in his old age.
> —Genesis 37:3 NLT

In each of these situations in the Bible there was trouble in the family because of favoritism. The Greek word for partial is *diakrino,* meaning to separate, distinguish, discern, judge, or decide. When we show partiality, we are judging. Oswald Chambers explains, "Beware of anything that puts you in the superior person's place. Stop having a measuring rod for other people. There is always one fact more in every man's case about which we know nothing."[2]

At the root of impartiality is a spirit of love. Jesus commanded to us to "love your neighbor as yourself" (Matthew 22:39 NLT). He also taught, "Do unto others as you would have them do unto you" (Matthew 7:12 NLT) and "I command you to love each other in the same way that I love you" (John 15:12 NLT).

Love is an attitude that shows in our actions. It is not a feeling. We don't have to feel guilty about not liking everybody. Jesus probably didn't like everyone with whom he came in contact—think about the Pharisees. I can obey Christ's command to love people I don't particularly like by treating them with respect. By acting unselfishly I will refuse to trample over other people. Each one of us is made in God's image.

Ask God to help you see people through his impartial eyes. He is not pleased when we show favoritism based on appearance. Neither your financial status nor your occupation impresses God. He's interested in your heart. Stop and thank him right now for loving us all equally no matter who we are.

Ask God to help you see people through his impartial eyes.

> The LORD your God is the God of gods and Lord of lords. He is the great God, mighty and awesome, who shows no partiality and takes no bribes.
> —Deuteronomy 10:17 NLT

I Praise You Because You Are Impartial!

To know what God thinks about favoritism read James 2:1-13.

Questions for Reflection

Were you ever in a situation where favoritism was shown? How did it make you feel?

What are some of the detrimental effects of showing favoritism?

What attitude is behind showing partiality?

What steps can you take to begin to see people through God's eyes?

Pray

Dear God, I am so thankful your love for me isn't affected by how I look on the outside. You love all of us the same and that gives me great security. Check my motives, Lord, and help me to be unselfish. Let your great love for me show in the way I treat other people. I love you. Amen.

Related Verses

I solemnly command you in the presence of God and Christ Jesus and the holy angels to obey these instructions without taking sides or showing special favor to anyone.

—I Timothy 5:21 NLT

I see very clearly that God doesn't show partiality. In every nation he accepts those who fear him and do what is right.

—Acts 10:34-35 NLT

Some of them were supposed to be important leaders, but I didn't care who they were. God doesn't have any favorites! None of these so-called special leaders added anything to my message.

—Galatians 2:6 CEV

Endnotes

Introduction

1. A.W. Tozer, *The Knowledge of the Holy*, HarperCollins Publishers, 1961, 2.
2. Ibid, viii.

Chapter 1: God Is Unchanging

1. A.W. Tozer, *The Attributes of God Vol. 2*, Christian Publications, Inc., 2001, 99.

Chapter 2: God Is Forgiving

1. J.I. Packer, *Knowing God*, InterVarsity Press 1973, 223.

Chapter 3: God Is Loving

1. J. I. Packer, *Knowing God*, 111.
2. *USA Today*, Gannett Co., Inc., December 23, 2005.

Chapter 4: God Is Faithful

1. A.W. Tozer, *The Knowledge of the Holy*, 81.

Chapter 5: God Is Omniscient

1. A.W. Tozer, *The Pursuit of God*, Christians Publications, Inc. 1982, 1993, 37.
2. Cynthia Heald, *A Woman's Journey to the Heart of God*, Thomas Nelson, Inc. 1997, 179.

Chapter 6: God Is Omnipotent

1. A.W. Tozer, *The Attributes of God Vol. 2*, 87.

Chapter 7: God Is Omnipresent

1. A.W. Tozer, *The Knowledge of the Holy*, 76.

Chapter 8: God Is Holy

1. A.W. Tozer, *The Knowledge of the Holy*, 105.
2. A.W. Tozer, *The Attributes of God Vol. 1*, Christian Publications 1997, 160.
3. Ibid, 172.
4. A.W. Tozer, *The Knowledge of the Holy*, HarperCollins, 1961, 106.

Chapter 9: God Is Compassionate

1. Chip Ingram, *God, As He Longs for You to See Him*, Baker Books, 2004, 184.
2. Lloyd John Ogilvie, *Autobiography of God*, Regal Books, 1979, 236.

Chapter 10: God Is Victorious

1. J.I. Packer, *Knowing God*, 264.

Chapter 11: God Is Just

1. J.I. Packer, *Knowing God*, 143.

Chapter 12: God Is Trustworthy

1. Oswald Chambers, *My Utmost for His Highest*, August 12.

Chapter 13: God Is Merciful

1. A.W. Tozer, *The Knowledge of the Holy*, 91.
2. A.W. Tozer, *The Attributes of God Vol. 1*, 82.
3. Ibid., 85.

Chapter 14: God Is Eternal

1. A.W. Tozer, *The Knowledge of the Holy*, 47.

Chapter 15: God Is Sovereign

1. Cynthia Heald, *A Women's Journey to the Heart of God*, 155.

Chapter 16: God Is Relational

1. J.I. Packer, *Knowing God*, 42.

Chapter 17: God Is All-Wise

1. A.W. Tozer, *The Knowledge of the Holy*, 60.

2   A.W. Tozer, *The Attributes of God*, Vol. 2, 124.
3. Ibid., 138.

Chapter 18: God Is Good

1. A.W. Tozer, *The Knowledge of the Holy*, 83.
2. J.I. Packer, *Knowing God*, 162.

Chapter 19: God Is Generous

1. J.I. Packer, *Knowing God*, 162.

Chapter 20: God Is Perfect

1. A.W. Tozer, *The Attributes of God*, Vol. 1, 186.

Chapter 21: God Is Truthful

1. J.I. Packer, *Knowing God*, 113.

Chapter 22: God Is Accessible

1. A.W. Tozer, *The Knowledge of the Holy*, 76.

Chapter 23: God Is Extravagant

1. A.W. Tozer, *The Knowledge of the Holy*, 93.

Chapter 24: God Is Loyal

1. Chip Ingram, *God As He Longs for You to See Him*, 210.

Chapter 25: God Is Gracious

1. Steve McVey, *Grace Rules*, Harvest House Publishers, 1998, 23.

Chapter 26: God Is Creative

1. A.W. Tozer, *The Attributes of God Vol. 2*, 57.

Chapter 27: God Is Majestic

1. J.I. Packer, *Knowing God*, 83.
2. Jane Szita, *Holland Herald*, Media Partners, February 2006, 33-34.

Chapter 28: God Is Infinite

1. A.W. Tozer, *The Knowledge of the Holy*, 13.

Chapter 29: God Is Patient

1. Oswald Chambers, *My Utmost for His Highest*, April 4.

Chapter 30: God Is Gentle

1. Cynthia Heald, *A Woman's Journey to the Heart of God*, 206.

Chapter 31: God Is Impartial

1. A.W. Tozer, *The Pursuit of God*, 62.
2. Oswald Chambers, *My Utmost for his Highest*, June 17.

All word definitions are from www.dictionary.com.

www.ingramcontent.com/pod-product-compliance
Lightning Source LLC
Chambersburg PA
CBHW030317080526
44584CB00012B/602